The Dynamics

of

CONFLICT

Knowledge for a Better Leadership

A Research Study

Njikang Clovis Mebinaji

ISBN:
ISBN-13: 978-4-9910517-1-5

DEDICATION

With deep affection and heartfelt gratitude,
this book is dedicated to

My beloved wife, Catherine Mebinaji
for always being by my side

And to

My daughter, Mebilyn.

CONTENTS

Acknowledgments   v

Chapter 1:   Introduction   1

Chapter 2:   A Review of the Nature & Concept of Conflict   10

Chapter 3:   The Genesis of Conflict   20

Chapter 4:   Conflict & Productivity   30

Chapter 5:   Conflict & Management Intervention   57

Chapter 6:   The Case Study   92

Chapter 7:   Conclusion & Recommendations   106

References   118

Appendix A – F   125

About The Author   137

ACKNOWLEDGMENTS

I would like to give all the glory to the Almighty God for inspiring and motivating me to write this book, my second publication. This book is designed for managers and leaders of organizations. I hope it will be a blessing.

I would also like to thank my beloved wife, Catherine Mebinaji. Thank you so much sweetheart for your moral and spiritual support. You made the environment comfortable for me to write this book. Without the environment you provided at home, the writing and publication of this book wouldn't have been possible. God bless you.

Finally, my gratitude to Emen Press for the publication of this book.

CHAPTER 1

INTRODUCTION

1.1 Why I Undertook This Research

It was the ancient Roman writer, Horace, who said the writing of a writer should be kept private for nine years before it can be unveiled to the general public. [1] This gives the writer enough time to test the validity of their material with respect to the audience to which it is written. That is, the nine year time frame gives the writer an opportunity to revisit the cases and arguments presented in their work and make changes that correspond to the changing society. My little fifteen year experience in the fields of business administration as well as Church administration and

---

[1] Marshal Sashkin and Molly G. Sashkin, *Leadership that Matters: The Critical Factors for Making a Difference in People's Lives and Organizations' Success* (USA: Berrett-Koehler Publishers, Inc., 2003), 1.

education combined has been that too often than not, the powers that be tend to turn a blind eye to the petty conflicts that arise among workers in organizations. They do this by harboring the false presumption that these conflicts have very little or no bearing with the organization's overall output. This research, which was undertaken in a glass processing factory located in the Saitama prefecture of Japan, will prove them wrong. It is a must-read document for managers and leaders who would like to optimize their production level.

I began gathering data and penning down my observations as far back as 2004, one year after I was employed as an accountant in the then largest cocoa/coffee trading company located in Douala, Cameroon, known as OLAM CAM Ltd.

In 2004 at OLAM CAM Ltd, after observing some negative work trends in my co-workers, which were as a result of the conflict they had with other co-workers - tearing them apart, altering their work focus, speed, and efficiency - I kept wondering as a young accountant why the conflicts were not resolved by top management as fast as anyone would have expected. What even surprised me the more was that the conflicts were not under any consideration as an issue to be tackled; they were totally disregarded as inconsequential to the firm's success. I thought it was a leadership weakness of the Finance Manager to whom we were all responsible. When a new Finance Manager was transferred into our company, he emulated the same attitude as the former one.

This made me to conclude that it was not just an issue of leadership weakness per se, but it seemed clearly to me it was the approach top management had adopted to handle conflict-relating issues: *outright negligence, warning and firing if conflict persists.* The best I could hear and see from a top management official after a conflict issue pitting my co-workers was the issuance of a communiqué of warning to the entire staff of that department. In the case of our department, this communiqué forbade us, particularly parties in conflict, from throwing words of insult at each other and from engaging in any act of violence within the company premises or during hours of its operations. It was a kind of leadership by suppression. This suppression even added more fuel to the issue concerned as it made other colleagues of mine complain quietly and bitterly about the arrogance of our boss. Some of them said they were going to leave the company for good.

Permit me mention, as an example of conflict, the case of Moses, a staff in our department. When Moses reported to the Finance Manager a conflict that had transpired for several weeks between him and the Accounts Supervisor, Moses was not only spoken harsh to, but was demoted straightaway before my eyes and given a warning of dismissal.

When I joined the company in March 2003, Moses was the one who had been assigned to train me on the job. I sat close to Moses for close to three months and saw how Moses became more depressed as the days went by. Moses' motivation to work gradually kept fading away. A handful of my colleagues and I were so perplexed with our boss' decision and attitude towards Moses.

It is with this respect that I decided to undergo a thorough research that looks at the role workplace conflict plays on the productivity of a worker and on the general long term stability of the organization. With regards to this subject, the chapters that would be presented reflect to a greater extent the writer's experiences of what conflict does and can do to any organization be they profit-making or not, be they stationed in the developed or developing world.

1.2 Research Background: Conflict, A Natural Phenomenon

As an individual draws up the boundaries of his soul, he establishes at the same time the battles of his soul.
- Ken Wilber, philosopher

When two or more organisms interact, whether they are humans, chimpanzees, baboons, tigers, buffalos, birds, or mice, they emit certain amount of energies (such as speech sounds, tones, body postures, odors, facial expressions, prejudices, etc), which react to define and shape their interrelation. The energy produced as a result may be socially favorable, socially unfavorable, or a blend of both. Worthy to note is that some of the interaction processes that take place around and within these individuals can be visible by our naked senses, while others, just like the reaction of molecules in matter, cannot. This invisible reaction process, which takes place within workers in conflict, is what Anolli et al. describe as "the hidden structure of interaction." [2] And this is what this book aims at bringing into the limelight so that leaders can be aware of and take immediate actions that will help to prevent their organizations from sinking deep.

As a leader, to not expect conflict of any nature, no matter how small, in your organization is a wish that should not be entertained especially owing to our fallen human nature and also due to socio-cultural differences. Your organization is often made up of individuals with different cultures, religions, races, preferences, etc. Each individual has their own lenses through which judgments are made regarding the actions of their leader and fellow workers. This tendency, by default, makes the non-occurrence of conflict an impossibility. Some workers deliberately hold firmly certain beliefs which they are not ready to let go for the sake of seeking the organizational goal. All these make conflicts in organizations imminent.

1.3 Thesis Statement

The thesis statement for this research shall be *Resolving workplace conflicts will booster the growth of your organization.*

---

[2] Luigi Anolli et al., eds., *The Hidden Structure of Interaction: From Neurons to Culture Patterns* (Amsterdam: IOS Press, 2005), 1-4.

1.4 Research Goals

1.4.1 Internal Goal: Finding Solutions to Research Problems

The primary goal of this project is to find out solutions to the problems that underlie this research, commonly known as *research problems*. These are stated here below:

1.4.1.1 Main Research Problems

- *Does workplace conflict hinder a worker's productivity?*

- *If yes, what should be done to prevent further loss in productivity?*

1.4.1.2 Subsidiary Research Problem

- *Can a workplace conflict contribute in any way to a worker's productivity?*

- *Should all workplace conflicts be addressed?*

1.4.2 External Goal: Corporate Leaders

The book aims at inviting and challenging leaders holding positions of responsibilities in organizations reflect on the issues presented, and take corrective measures to restore serenity so that the worker and the leader who manages the organization's affairs can both enjoy the mutual benefit of co-operation: A decrease in the burden of the worker leads to a corresponding decrease in the intervention of the leader; a decrease in the worker's burden leads to a greater commitment, which ultimately leads to an increase in output and stability of the organization.

Moreover, this writer will be highlighting the impact workplace conflict plays on the organization on a social and judicial level. This fact seems to have escaped the attention of most leaders in decision-making positions today. This ailment (conflict) that disrupts the work process and an effective administration of business travels a long way to denounce an organization to its stakeholders for not being a true apostle of employee welfare. Conflict, no matter the scale, is a precursor of the potential detriment that could befall an organization if no immediate actions are taken.

1.5 Assumptions of Study

This project, like any science, operates under a number of assumptions laid down here-below:

- All workplace-related conflicts have their roots in the workplace. Thus, they are created by the system or people who function in that system.

- These conflicts push the affected workers into a 'depressive state.'

- The organization concerned has no established structure for handling matters relating to workplace conflicts.

1.6 Defining "Productivity"

Generally, productivity could be defined as "the efficient use of resources – labor, capital, land, materials, energy, information – in the production of various goods and services."[3]

Simply stated,   Productivity $= \dfrac{\text{Output}}{\text{Input}}$

Worker A, for example, is said to be more productive than worker B when A, using the same amount of resources (input) as B, produces more results (output) than B.

For simplicity, we define *productivity* here as the amount and 'quality' of work done by an employee over a time *t* that is reminiscent of the *wages* he/she earns, which we will refer to as *compensation*. This *productivity* may either fall below or above the compensation line. For the company to survive, the commitment of her employees must at least meet certain standards both in magnitude and quality. So, by *sustainable productivity*, we mean a work performance that hits, by all possible means, the compensation line, or any point above it.

Other terms used in the project will be duly defined.

---

[3] Joseph Prokopenko, *Productivity Management: A Practical Handbook* (Geneva: Int'l Labour Office, 1987), 3.

1.7 Disposition of Thesis

This book is made up of seven chapters. Chapter 1 (current) deals with the Introduction. The various themes of the remaining chapters are listed as follows: Chapter 2 - Literature Review; Chapter 3 – Conflict and Productivity, Chapter 4 – Conflict and Management Intervention; Chapter 5 – Research Methodology; Chapter 6 – Case Study; Chapter 7 – Conclusion and Recommendations.

HISTORICAL REVIEW of CONFLICT

Winston Churchill once said: *The further backward you can look the farther forward you are likely to see.* In order to go ahead devising ways of carrying out this research project effectively, we would need to, first of all, halt, make a U-turn, and look backwards for a while considering any useful scholarly literature relating to the subject of conflict. Since any credible academic writing must take into account the already existing literature (textbooks, journal articles, website publications, etc.) that relates to the current research, this section of the project is dedicated to examining the body of academic writing that relates to our project and that will provide us with the necessary concepts, theories, and models that might guide our current research.

2.2 Conflict: Concept & Theories

Conflict is a reality that had long existed, and that continues to exist, in the human society today – both formal and informal. Conflict is not only born by us, it is as well borne by us when we sacrifice the common goal for our personal ambitions. Philosophy and sociology are two of the major disciplines that have made significant contributions to the theory and practice of social conflict.

2.2.1 Plato and Aristotle

From philosophy, both Plato and Aristotle saw the backlash of conflict within a society and advocated for societal order. [4] For Plato, since it is natural for some tension to exist within a society, conflicts are inevitable. "However, he felt that if a proper balance of the parts could be obtained, social conflict could be at a minimum. Each segment of society must know the part it must play and be guided in such a fashion that all segments work together in harmony" (Schellenberg, 1996: 89). [5] And appropriate leadership is the way suggested by Plato for obtaining the proper balance of the parts.

In *The Republic,* Plato submitted that the needs of every society could

____

[4] M. Afzalur Rahim, ed., *Managing Conflict in Organizations* (USA: Greenwood Publishing Group, 2001), 2.
[5] Ibid.

be satisfied only when private property is eliminated. [6] Thus, when private interests do interplay and the result does not promote or contribute to the accomplishment of group goals, a conflict is born. Conflict, therefore, does not exist until parties assigned to a common task begin to look out for personal interests. Thus, the absence of conflict, Plato and Aristotle did stress, is a sine qua non for the achievement of societal goals. For these philosophers, "strife is a sign of imperfection and unhappiness. Order marks the good life and disorders the opposite. Conflict is a threat to the success of the state and should be kept at an absolute minimum, and removed altogether if possible" (Sipka, 1969: 7). [7]

2.2.2 Thomas Hobbes (1588-1679) & John Locke (1632-1704)

The social contract theories of Thomas Hobbes and John Locke suggest that in social relations, strife between humans is not absent, and that the role of the government is therefore to reduce such strife by establishing order without which there would be constant chaos. [8] For Lourenco and Glidewell (1975:489), Hobbes saw humans as "egotistical, the dupes of error, the slaves of sin, of passion, and of fear. Persons are their own enemies, or the enemies of others, or both." [9]

---

[6] Ibid.
[7] Rahim, 3.
[8] Ibid.
[9] Ibid.

It is important to note that, Sipka writes, both:

> Hobbes and Locke had an extraordinary sensitivity to the dangers of social conflict and sought, through government, to control it as much as possible….not only did these men not see a growth or re-constructive potential in social conflict, but they considered it a flaw in the body politic…. Though neither man insists that all conflict is to be removed, it is clear that this is their intention (Sipka, 1969: 15-16). [10]

2.2.3 Elton Mayo (1880-1949)

Moving to the discipline of sociological sciences, we encounter the Australian-born sociologist and organization theorist, Elton Mayo, whose works revolutionized the social conflict theory and brought about the human relations movement. To improve organizational effectiveness, Mayo stressed, cooperation is necessary. Mayo saw social conflict as an evil that hampers organizational effectiveness and advocated that it be minimized or eliminated altogether, if possible. [11] In his 1995 publication (p. 88-9), Child concluded that Mayo had a:

> Deep abhorrence of conflict in any form…. Mayo and his colleagues…assumed that ordinary

---

[10] Rahim, 3.
[11] Ibid., 6.

employees were largely governed by a "logic of sentiment," which was of a different order from managers' rational appraisal of the situation in terms of costs and efficiency. Conflict with management was thus an aberration that threatened the effectiveness of organizations. [12]

2.2.4 De Borno

A prolific writer on social conflict to mention here is De Borno (1986). For De Borno, to resolve a conflict means to eliminate the conflict entirely. De Borno coined the terms "confliction" meaning "to create conflict," and "de-confliction" meaning "to eliminate conflict."

> De-confliction does not refer to negotiation or bargaining or even to the resolution of conflicts. De-confliction is the effort required to evaporate a conflict. Just as confliction is the setting up of a conflict so de-confliction is the opposite process: the demolition of the conflict (De Borno, 1986: 5). [13]

2.3 Conflict: Definition & Practice

---

[12] Rahim, 6
[13] Ibid., 13.

> The picture of the great corporation as a peaceful cooperative of its participants is more than highly improbable, it is extraordinarily fraudulent. The modern corporation is socially a theatre of all the conflicts that might be expected when hundreds and thousands of highly charged, exceptionally self-motivated, and more than normally, self-serving people work closely together (Galbraith, 1986: 21). [14]

It may not surprise you to know that many authors differ in how they view and define conflict. Some view conflict as "a struggle over values and claims to scarce status, power, and resources, a struggle in which the aims of opponents are to neutralize, injure, or eliminate rivals" (Lewis Coser); [15] others view the same as the perception of differences and opposition in beliefs and values between an individual or group and another individual or group (De Dreu et al., 1999; Wall & Callister, 1995). [16] For Fink (1968), conflict is "any social situation or process in which two or more social entities are linked by at least one form of antagonistic psychological relation or at least one form of antagonistic interaction." [17] To add to these, we can define conflict as a situation

---

[14] Deborah Kolb and Jean Bartunek, eds., *Hidden Conflict in Organizations: Uncovering Behind-the-Scenes Disputes* (California: Sage Publications Inc., 1992), 1.

[15] Kevin Avruch, *Culture and Conflict Resolution* (Washington: United States Institute of Peace Press, 1998), 24.

[16] Carsten K. W. De Dreu and Bianca Beersma, eds., *Conflict in Organizations: Beyond Effectiveness and Performance* (UK: Psychology Press Ltd., 2005), 106.

whereby an actor uses a socio-cultural advantage to suppress or oppress a rival or any person that challenges the actor's position.

However, our working definition for workplace conflict shall be stated as follows: *Any organizational event that subjects an individual or group either mentally, psychologically or physically to an extreme feeling of rejection, dejection, unjustness, bias, or abuse, and which potentially hinders the progress of the individual (or group) towards achieving a goal.*

Glancing through the manuscript of "Leading through Conflict" by Mark Gerzon, a senior sales manager of a world-renown computer company said he was not quite interested in the book for conflict was not an issue in their company. When asked how he did define conflict, the executive said, "People shouting and calling each other names." Then turning towards Gerzon, the executive asks, "How do you define it?" "Conflict," Gerzon replies, "is anything that results in chronic inefficiency for the system of which it is a part." Because this definition was functional and task-oriented, it allowed the executive grasp the integral nature of conflict and relate to it vividly like never before. Having been enlightened, the executive then confessed of several off-the-scene conflicts that had been taking place in their company, [18] which they had ignored.

---

[17] Anne Maydan Nicotera, ed., *Conflict and Organizations: Communicative Processes* (Albany: State University of New York Press, 1995), 5.
[18] Mark Gerzon, *Leading through Conflict: How Successful Leaders Transform Differences into Opportunities* (USA: Harvard Business School Press, 2006), 34.

Most managers are yet to grasp the integral nature of conflicts, their causes, and consequences on company growth. Some have even turned a blind eye to specific conflicts to the detriment of the organization's success. When conflicts are ignored, the affected employees, and hence the organization as a whole, suffer.

A 2004 report by the Economic Intelligence Unit Survey reveals that out of the 11 million corporate meetings that are held in a day, more than half are considered a poor use of time by their participants. [19] One of the reasons for this deficiency, Gerzon argues, is the omission of conflicts in board meetings. Workplace conflicts, Gerzon continues, the real challenges that managers face today, are either mishandled or avoided in these meetings altogether. "Both," talking about mishandling and avoidance, "can significantly compromise productivity," [20] he added.

2.4 Types of Conflict

No matter what they are, conflicts that occur within the walls of an organization generally fall under the following categories: *intrapersonal, interpersonal, intragroup,* or *intergroup conflicts.* [21]

1. Intrapersonal Conflict

Also known as *intraindividual* or *intrapsychic conflict,* this

---

[19] Gerzon, 34.
[20] Ibid.
[21] Rahim, 23.

category of conflict is used to describe conflict that occurs within an individual. Such a conflict occurs when an individual is torn between incompatible goals (Coombs and Avrunin, 1983: 7). It may occur, for example, when a worker is assigned to a task that does not represent his area of expertise, goals, or values of interests. [22] Conflicts that fall within this category are often hard to trace and therefore hard to resolve. However, they provide important guidelines to tackling other forms of conflicts. Understanding the plight of an individual and the conditions that must be in place for the conflict within that individual to be deescalated has valuable applications to conflicts between individuals. [23]

2. Interpersonal Conflict

If you had read a few job advertisements, or attended some interviews, you should have realized by now that amongst the requirements expected from potential job candidates, good *interpersonal skills* are often stressed the most. The emphasis on interpersonal skills is not just for formality sake. Rather, companies have increasingly become conscious of the impact of these skills in the day-to-day affairs of their businesses.

Also known as *dyadic conflict,* interpersonal conflicts are those

---

[22] Rahim, 23

[23] Clyde H. Coombs and George S. Avrunin, *The Structure of Conflict* (New Jersey: Lawrence Erlbaum Associates, Inc., 1988), 11.

conflicts that occur between two or more individuals occupying the same or different levels of organizational hierarchy. Conflicts between coworkers, for example, and those involving superiors and their subordinates fall under this category. [24]

3. Intragroup Conflict

Also known as *intradepartmental conflict*, this category embodies conflicts that occur within a group or sub-groups of an organizational department. These conflicts are principally related to issues such as the nature of tasks, procedures, goals, etc. [25]

4. Intergroup Conflict

Also known as *interdepartmental conflict,* this category is comprised of conflicts that transpire between two or more groups or departments of an organization having distinct functions. They include conflicts between departments such as Procurement and Production, Auditing and Accounting, Marketing and Sales, to name these few. [26]

2.5 Depression, a Side Effect of Conflict

Most of us frequently use the word *depression* in common speech to refer to situations that cause extreme pain, sorrow, and loss. These situations, which usually come and go, have their roots in our social interactions with others. Hence, the use of the term *depressed worker* in this project takes this sense. It does not in any way refer to a

---

[24] Rahim, 23.
[25] Rahim, 23-24.
[26] Ibid., 24.

worker who has been diagnosed with having a clinical depression. While the form of depression discussed in this project, let us call it *social depression*, is a normal human condition, clinical depression, also known as *affective disorders*, is not normal at any stage of the human life. [27]

---

[27] Jacquelin Berman and Lisa M. Furst, *Depressed Older Adults: Education and Screening* (New York: Springer Publishing Company, LLC, 2011), 2.

THE GENESIS OF CONFLICT

3.1 The Comfort Zone Theory

While the primary ingredients in any conflict are the individuals involved, conflicts tend to spring from the same litany of sources for all people, and virtually every conflict begins with someone or something violating an individual's "comfort zone."

Each of us defines our "comfort zone" by erecting limits on what we perceive to be acceptable, allowable, "safe" experiences and behaviors. Any event that intrudes, threatens or assaults our comfort zone, or requires us to move beyond the limits of our

> comfort zone, produces conflict. Our first awareness
> of conflict comes from the feelings that are produced
> when the comfort zone is violated – David Cowan. [28]

The concept of "comfort zone" has a very profound significance to the animal class in general, and to us humans, in particular. As we grow from infancy through adolescence to adulthood in our respective communities, and as we study along in various public, private, and religious institutions, and hang out with various people, we embrace certain values we so much cherish while rejecting those we find strange and unfriendly. The set of values we have embraced over the years is what has defined our personality today – who we really are - which in other words could be collectively described as our *comfort zone.* "The stronger the belief or the more important the value," Cowan writes, "the greater the discomfort and attendant conflict." [29]

As we dialogue and work with other people, especially those from an entirely different background, we keep a keen watch on our comfort zone. Anyone who makes an attempt to forcefully hijack us away from our comfort zone by either influencing or forcing us act in ways not prescribed by our comfort zone is immediately perceived as an enemy. As such, such a person must be dealt with

---

[28] David Cowan, *Taking Charge of Organizational Conflict: A Guide to Managing Anger and Confrontation* (USA: Personhood Press, 2003), 13.
[29] Ibid., 15.

or avoided altogether.

In my experience and study of organizational behavior, I have discovered that, among others, workers have three key values they so much treasure such that when one of them is violated, the worker somehow becomes emotionally displaced, which may lead to depression if appropriate care is not taken. These three constitute the comfort zone of the worker, or, to use David Cowan's term, the worker's "hot buttons". They are, in ascending order: (1) The need to be talked to, (2) The need to be respected and valued, and most importantly (3) The need to be in control (autonomy).

Pyramid Showing the Three Key Values of
a Worker's "Comfort Zone"

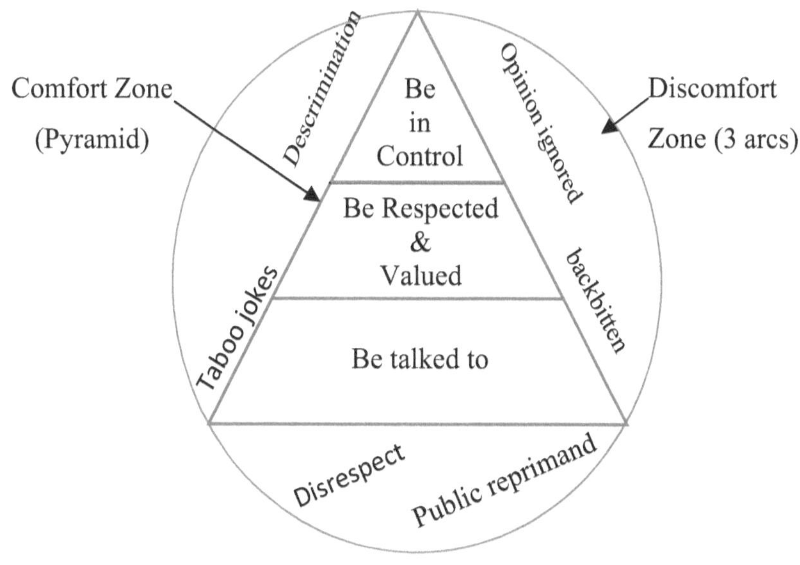

The Three Key Values of a Worker

1. The Need to be talked to

At the base of the worker's comfort zone lies the worker's need to be talked to by fellow co-workers. Every worker uses this mechanism to judge whether he/she is accepted by co-workers or not. When a worker senses that they are always left alone while other colleagues get along so well, they feel a deep sense of rejection. Sooner or later, the worker concerned gradually develops a negative feeling towards co-workers for comfort zone violation. This seems to be a natural process that occurs within every worker who experiences isolation irrespective of the awareness of comfort zone violators.

It seems to me that even workers who hardly talk to people hold this need in high esteem. One day, I decided to initiate a casual dialogue with a co-worker of reserved character who was working in another unit of our department. Both of us had met several times without having any amicable discussion. To my greatest astonishment, the person I thought was reserved almost sounded to me like a Sunday School teacher as he began briefing and advising me on how to deal with certain work processes, which I had limited knowledge of. The conversation I thought would end in a "Hello-Hello" fashion ended up in a warm and exciting way. That was because someone's comfort zone was respected when he was talked to. So, when we talk to the people who work in our organizations, we make them feel at home and wanted. This boosts their morale and prevents potential conflicts.

2. The Need to be Respected & Valued

Even though most of the time we fail to acknowledge the offices of our leaders and the experiences of veteran workers, and give these people the respect they deserve, we always want our efforts to be noticed, and we want to be respected by everyone for our contributions. Probably, we could say this is a human default characterized by our attitude of self-center.

Once the need *to be talked to* is violated, it most often leads the worker to conclude they are not being respected and valued by the violator. Workers generally perceive co-workers who do not respect and value them as enemies though in the same team.

Regarding valuation, it seems to me that the plight of every worker is "to be recognized" and "appreciated" by the organization's management and fellow co-workers. A worker is valued when their services are regarded to be most productive, and forms a significant contribution to the company growth. When a worker does not receive from management commendation for a job well done, they feel undervalued (comfort zone of "being valued" violated) and gradually they begin to develop some negative attitudes towards work and management. This reduces the worker's input, and, hence, the organization's growth.

Work Harassment

One major area in the workplace where workers have often felt disrespected and undervalued is work harassment by staff who are either in the management bench or are simply older in the organization than the marginalized workers.

A deep reflection on human activity throughout history, a master-slave relationship, reveals that most workers were dissatisfied with the way they were treated by their masters, with the masters taking advantage of their privileged positions to suppress them. Today, this trend still exists in many organizations.

In most cases, the slaves had to work under inhumane conditions with little or no security. Having no formal platform to lay their grievances, the slaves had no choice but to succumb to the ill-treatment meted out to them:

> While the problem of humanization has always, from an axiological point of view, been humankind's central problem, it now takes on the character of an inescapable concern. Concern for humanization leads at once to the recognition of dehumanization, not only as an ontological possibility but as an historical reality. [30]

And fragments of this historical reality are very much alive in our society today, if not in their crooked form, at least in modernized and politicized forms. Due to today's ever-changing economic trends, employment crisis seems to be the biggest social problem in developing countries. And employers are taking advantage of this crisis to institute in their organizations rules and practices of labor that are not in conformity with local and international norms, knowing that their workers would have no choice but to comply. The same spirit of subjection flows down the veins of the organization's hierarchy – leaders suppress their subordinates, and established employees suppress new ones. And this weighs terribly on the shoulders of the affected persons in particular, and on the organization's success in general.

In other countries, it is the problem of taking advantage of others through cultural norms. This is common in Japan where most workers do not leave their workplaces even after their official working time is over. They must not leave while the company president is still in office. I have heard many of my Japanese colleagues complain silently about this with no one daring to question this work injustice. Worthy to note is that according to the Japanese culture, the society functions as a group with members taking exclusive instructions for group operations from their leader without questioning the leader's decision.

---

[30] Paulo Freire, *Pedagogy of the Oppressed: 30th Anniversary Edition,* trans. Myra Bergman Ramos (New York: Continuum Int'l Pub. Group Inc., 2006), 43.

It is for this reason that this project holds the view that *Workers, irrespective of the industry, are in some kind of conflicts exerted on them by their manager or by fellow co-workers, and would become more productive only when these conflicts are resolved.* This statement constitutes the thesis of this project.

But while both humanization and dehumanization are real alternatives, only the first is the people's vocation. This vocation is constantly negated, yet it is affirmed by that very negation. It is thwarted by injustice, exploitation, oppression, and the violence of the oppressors; it is affirmed by the yearning of the oppressed for freedom and justice, and by their struggle to recover their lost humanity. [31]

A research conducted by the Marshall School of Business in the University of Southern California reveals that four out of every five employees feel disrespected at work. And a majority alluded to the progressive rise of conflicts in their organizations. In addition, the average manager of a large company spends at least seven weeks a year attending to workplace conflicts. [32]

3. The Need to be in Control

The need to be in control means the need to feel like we are in control of ourselves and our destiny – that

---

[31] Freire, 43-44.
[32] Ibid., 34.

we have options, and that we are free and able to make choices. Whenever we sense that we are, or are about to be, out of control, we experience discomfort proportional to the extent of the loss. Severe discomfort and, consequently, intense conflict can result. [33]

The need to be in control is the greatest and most sensitive of the three. The worker can move on when the need *to be talked to* and the need *to be valued and respected* are violated, but as soon as their autonomy is tempered with, there is a swift physical reaction. This reaction can take the form of verbal agitations (rare in Eastern countries, especially Japan) or a sudden change of mood (mostly common).

My experience of working with people from different nationalities, race, gender, and age groups in the past fifteen years has revealed one common predominant factor: *the need to be in control of oneself and one's operations*. And this principle seems to hold true even in circumstances when the worker is incompetent in handling basic elements of organizational operations. In order to abide in their comfort zone of *being in control*, most employees accept job offers and tasks only to submit their inability to do the said tasks after a series of failures.

In 2004, I was assigned to train a fresh graduate who had just been

---

[33] Cowan, 14.

accepted into our company (OLAM CAM Ltd.) on the management of cash and stock operations using the company's software. This operation usually took workers on average six weeks for complete mastery. After two weeks of training, the new recruit, thinking he had already mastered the system, began paying less attention to me. He felt he was ripe enough to command the operation; he wanted to be in full control of the operation just after receiving a few lessons of introduction. Despite the fact that the young man was smart per se, I felt he still needed to be taken through some complex operations, especially those relating to the central warehouse management and government taxes, which had not yet been treated.

CHAPTER 4

CONFLICT & PRODUCTIVITY

4.1 How Does Being Depressed Affect Productivity?

For this demonstration, we will use conflict as our source of depression. When a conflict springs up, it injects its poisonous venom into its captive. This venom bruises the captive's motivation to work, turning the captive into a spirit of *depression*, animosity, disconsolation, vengeance, dolor, rancor, and bloodthirstiness.

> Though with their high wrongs I am struck to th'quick ,
> Yet with my nobler reason 'gainst my fury
> Do I take part (Shakespeare, *The Tempest)*.

As a result, the disabled motivation of the captive worker is unable to attain the level of production it used to. The disability deteriorates to a point where the captive, becoming fully aware of his inability to perform as required, and of his incapacity to overcome the situation, decides to seek for managerial solution or quit entirely.

Commenting on the destructive nature of conflict, Neuhauser (1988: 3) writes,

> "Conflict is a major source of increased stress and decreased productivity for all managers and employees in any department of any organization. It almost always ends up affecting the quality of services received by customers." [34]

Statistics show that out of ten employees, more than half report of having "lost work time" due to conflicts. More than one out of the ten have actually quit their jobs as a result of conflict mismanagement. [35]

4.2 Conflict Affects Productivity: A Scientific Proof

To prove that conflict depression does affect productivity, we must first establish the case that conflicts are real and that they are a natural human phenomenon. To achieve this first task, we will look

---

[34] Cowan, 12.
[35] Gerzon, 35.

at the famous work of Charles Darwin.

4.3 Charles Darwin & the theory of *Survival of the Fittest*

In his *The Origin of Species by Means of Natural Selection*, a work considered to be the foundation of evolutionary biology, Charles Darwin (1809-82), after an extensive research on the evolution of species (both animals and plants), came up with the finding that due to the geometrical increase in organic beings coupled with the limited number of resources, each species, in the struggle for survival, becomes naturally competitive and aggressive, resulting to an outbreak of war between species. [36]

Expanding further, Darwin comments:

> But the struggle will almost invariably be most severe between the individuals of the same species, for they frequent the same districts, require the same food, and are exposed to the same dangers. In the case of varieties of the same species, the struggle will generally be almost equally severe, and we sometimes see the contest soon decided: for instance, if several varieties of wheat be sown together, and the mixed seed be resown, some of the varieties which best suit the soil or climate, or are

------

[36] Charles Darwin, *The Origin of Species by Means of Natural Selection* (Madison: Cricket House Books, LLC, 2010), 48.

naturally the most fertile, will beat the others and so yield more seed, and will consequently in a few years supplant the other varieties.... So again with the varieties of sheep: it has been asserted that certain mountain-varieties will starve out other mountain-varieties, so that they cannot be kept together. [37]

Thus conflicts are real. They are a predicament we have to bear as part of our existence. Except for peculiar cases, conflicts are, generally speaking, not a desired human phenomenon. They are simply injuries we afflict or are afflicted by others in the process of acquiring our desires. Having established this first case, we shall move further into the crux of the matter: *proving being depressed affects productivity.*

Note that, as we had clearly stated above, the potential outcome of conflict is depression. And a depressive state, which represents, to use the words of Price et al., "a psycho-biological response pattern of the human organism," [38] is, I suppose, generally counter-productive. In support of this hypothesis, Radford et al. (1986) write, "Performance is limited in depression. *There is impairment of perception, of execution and of the central processes which mediate between perception and execution*, experienced as

---

[37] Darwin, 48.
[38] Simon Baron-Cohen (ed.), *The Maladapted Mind: Classic Readings in Evolutionary Psychopathology* (UK: Psychology Press, 1997), 241.

difficulty in making decisions" [39] (italics added). Thus, depression, which is again identified by Price et al. as "a losing or de-escalating strategy," [40] limits productivity. But how does this really happen? To show this further, we shall briefly consult the field of Cognitive Neuroscience.

4.4 Cognitive Neuroscience – A Short View

Remember that Aristotle divided the mind into three functions or domains: Cognition, Emotion, and Collation (or will). And we are told that Emotion has the power to guide, influence, or constrain mental functions that are indisputably cognitive such as memory, attention, and perception. [41] For the sake of this project, we would need to specifically define what an emotion is. We shall consider the psychologist view. For psychologists, Parrott writes, emotions are simply "ongoing states of mind that are marked by mental, bodily, or behavioral symptoms." [42]

Therefore, if the worker's emotion (assuming it is depressive) is capable of constraining the worker's memory, attention, and perception, as mentioned above, it goes without saying that such a worker would remain unproductive at the workplace as long as the

---

[39] Ibid., 241.
[40] Baron-Cohen, 242.
[41] Richard D. Lane and Lynn Nadel, eds., *Cognitive Neuroscience of Emotion:* (New York: Oxford University Press, Inc., 2000), 4.
[42] W. Gerrod Parrott, ed., *Emotions in Social Psychology: Essential Readings* (USA: Psychology Press, 2001), 3.

emotion or the social problem does persist.

4.5 Reasons Why Conflicts Have Skyrocketed

My experience in dealing with all kinds of organizations; big and small, public and private, and for profit and nonprofit, leads me to believe that, more and more, organizations are in the conflict business - not by choice, but certainly to the detriment of almost everything else they are trying to accomplish – David Cowan [43]

Below are some of the major reasons why conflict has gained too much resistance and control into our business organizations, and society in general.

1. Conflict Illiteracy

The question to ponder is, "Why has conflict gained too much roots and resistance into our businesses today?" Why do we still struggle with how to handle or address any sort of conflict? This social evil has permeated every sector of our society destabilizing it, transforming it, or extinguishing it altogether. It has transformed our marriages into divorces; our parliaments into boxing rings;

---

[43] Cowan, 4.

bilateral relationships between countries into cold wars; friendships into enmities; our peaceful streets into arenas of mass protests; productivity in organizations into unproductivity; employment into unemployment; to name these few. The answer to the above question is given by Mark Gerzon: a very large proportion of our generation is conflict illiterate. [44] In our schools we are taught how to take care of the environment, how to be a good citizen, how to keep fit to maintain a healthy life, but we are never taught how to handle situations of conflict. Rare to find in our universities, Gerzon argues, are courses on conflict and negotiation. These courses, if taught, are only offered as extracurricular modules, Gerzon added. So, "many students learn nothing about communicating across differences. If they do, it is often in a 'debate club,' which reinforces the pro/con, either/or way of experiencing differences." [45] The individual abilities of workers to successfully resolve conflict, David Cowan argues, has a direct link to the quality of conflict management at the organizational level. [46] But how can they manage an issue when they got no tools in their hands? It seems to me that even employers of labour have become aware of this human crisis that they find testing or assessing candidates' abilities to manage conflict an unnecessary venture.

---

[44] Gerzon, 227.
[45] Ibid.
[46] Cowan, 25.

In today's organizations, it is not enough to have job-related skills. It has become vitally important for people to acquire the skills necessary to successfully interact with others and to positively influence organizational culture. Too often we assume employees already possess these skills when, in fact, they don't. [47]

2. Worldview Intolerance

Moreover, another important reason for conflict is the problem of intolerance of the belief system of others. No man comes into this world with a specific worldview in mind; rather each of us is taught how to perceive the world. And one of the very first institutions we get such teachings from is religion. For simplicity, we would mention the three major religions. In Judaism, students are taught a worldview from a strictly Jewish perspective that is based on their precious Torah; in Christianity they are taught the Christian worldview based on their Holy Bible; and in Islam these students are radically groomed to see the world exclusively through the pages of their sacred Koran, marginalizing the other groups and baptizing them as *infidels*. In addition, even members of the same religion are further divided by race, region, tribe, culture, and language, parameters that have, to a greater extent, limited their scope of action towards outsiders.

---

[47] Cowan, 6.

What are we but sedition? like this poor France, faction against faction, within ourselves, every piece playing every moment its own game, with as much difference between us and ourselves as between ourselves and others. Whoever will look narrowly into his own bosom will hardly find himself twice in the same condition. I give to myself sometimes one face and sometimes another, according to the side I turn to. I have nothing to say of myself, entirely and without qualification (Montaigne, in Walter Pater, *Gaston de Latour*).

Thus, there is a very high conflict potential, *a conflict of worldviews*, which already exists amongst members of these groups. Remember that today there are over sixty-three thousand transnational companies with over eight hundred thousand subsidiaries flooding our planet employing more than 90 million people [48] each of whom is a product of the philosophical mindset of one of the defined groups mentioned above.

So, these people, after becoming employees of corporations, would ultimately react harshly and profusely to any sorts of conflict that threatens their ideological stand. As mentioned above, because they are unable to deal with this precarious situation due to conflict illiteracy, the crisis persists and develops further. The result is

---

[48] Cowan, 3.

internal unrest and a slow-down or boycott of organizational commitment. This therefore calls for an urgent managerial intervention. *It is for this reason that liberation leadership should be the model form of leadership for sustaining company growth through the elimination of adverse growth factors.* To add, when a conflict erupts unexpectedly, victimized employees do not have the time to consult a book that teaches the steps to be taken to quench or suppress the venom of conflict. Such employees, therefore, are in dire need of the emancipative action of their leader.

3. The Human Pride

It is no more big news that the fundamental problem we humans face today is self-pride. We want to correct others but we do not want to be corrected. Even though we are followers yet we want to lead; we do not want to be led. Even when we are less knowledgeable about a work process, we still fear being directed by a superior or coworker who has a better experience of the process than us. We claim and affirm we understand a process, but in reality we do not. We vehemently hesitate to give to Caesar what is Caesar's. However, we seek the recognition, approval and praises of others even in the things we know we least deserve. This is the human pride, a force in the being that sees itself as the supreme in terms of wisdom, knowledge, intelligence, creativity, beauty, race, kindness, consideration, compassion, generosity, courage, diplomacy, dynamism, diligence, prudence, exuberance, faithfulness, friendliness, gentleness, impartiality, modesty, patience, discipline, sincerity, and you name the rest. This pride therefore sets the man/woman high above others on a pedestal. So, any action (such as correction, hailing, rebuke) proceeding from others that reflect others' superiority over the man/woman in question is immediately met with objection irrespective of the way the action was communicated.

The human pride was identified by the 4th/5th century theologian, St. Augustine of Rome, as the major problem that is responsible for the fall and decay of the human race. This position, known as the Augustinian tradition, holds that because we chose not to obey our Creator, we make ourselves the center of our existence:

> Ignoring our Creator, we egocentrically attempt to control reality. We think more highly of ourselves than is warranted. From this angle, grandiosity is the self's nagging tendency. Conceit and arrogance are natural outgrowths of not realizing our limitations in relationship to our Source as well as others. [49]

4. The Human Idols

Francis Bacon, the prominent English philosopher of the 16th/17th century, considered one of the greatest thinkers the world has ever

---

[49] Terry D. Cooper, *Sin, Pride & Self-Acceptance: The Problem of Identity in Theology & Psychology* (USA: Inter Varsity Press, 2003), 7.

had, uses the symbolism of the 'Idols' or 'Illusions' to describe the fundamental defaults in men and in their relations with others, which lead these men to poor judgment of events thereby giving rise to chaos. These are the deep-seated causes of human misconception and irrationality. In his famous book, *The New Organon (Novum Organum,* in Latin), Bacon enumerates four idols that interfere with the processes of clear human reasoning and judgment. These include: *Idols of the Tribe, Idols of the Cave, Idols of the Marketplace,* and *Idols of the Theatre.* [50]

i. Idols of the Tribe (*Idola tribus*)

These are delusions or illusions or, simply put, false impressions that are embedded in the very human nature. These idols are associated with the specific race, gender, region, social class, etc to which men identify themselves. These idols have been shaped from history by the men and women of each tribe and have been passed from one generation to another, which has become the norm for sense perception and common practice for all members belonging to that tribe.

> Such then are the idols which I call *Idols of the Tribe*, and which take their rise either from the homogeneity of the substance of the human spirit, or from its preoccupation, or from its narrowness, or

---

[50] Francis Bacon, *The New Organon,* eds. Lisa Jardine and Michael Silverthorne (UK: Cambridge University Press, 2000), xix.

from its restless motion, or from an infusion of the affections, or from the incompetency of the senses, or from the mode of impression. [51]

ii. Idols of the Cave (*Idola specus*)

Unlike *Idols of the Tribe, Idols of the Cave* are illusions that are traceable to a particular individual and which hinder that individual's objective assessment of life issues. Within each tribe every individual has his/her own specific cave or den which scatters and discolours the light of nature. These illusions come about as a result of the person's individual nature and as a result of his/her unique experiences obtained from daily life. An employee who has been racially victimized in the past on several occasions would find it difficult to work amicably with a coworker of the opposite race. Tensions would be high and the probability of conflict emersion too would be high due to the constant vibration of the idols of prejudice in the employee's cave that impairs the employee's objective assessment of the present circumstance.

The *Idols of the Cave* take their rise in the peculiar constitution, mental or bodily, of each individual; and also in education, habit and accident. Of this kind there

---

[51] Francis Bacon, *The New Organon: The True Directions Concerning the Interpretations of Nature, LII, available from* http://books.google.co.jp/books?id=hTbE_UHvWg8C&printsec=frontcover#v=onepage&q&f=false

is a great number and variety. But I will instance those the pointing out of which contains the most important caution, and which have most effect in disturbing the clearness of the understanding…. There are found some minds given to an extreme admiration of antiquity, others to an extreme love and appetite for novelty; but few so duly tempered that they can hold the mean, neither carping at what has been well laid down by the ancients, nor despising what is well introduced by the moderns. [52]

iii. Idols of the Marketplace (*Idola fori*)

These are idols that are formed as men engage with one another either for common or unrelated goals. Men interact through the medium of conversation. But the conversation itself is simply an embodiment of words that are applied according to the capacity of the parties in conversation. The intelligence and capacity of the understanding and usage of conversation words of one party may be higher than the other party who may accuse the former of wrongdoings due to his/her idols of the Marketplace – inability to grasp the meaning of words. Because we humans reason through the meanings of words, Bacon affirms, this can be dangerous when the received words are given a false interpretation. This idol,

---

[52] Francis Bacon, *The New Organon: The True Directions Concerning the Interpretations of Nature,* LIII-LVI.

Bacon identifies as the most problematic of all.

> But the *Idols of the Market Place* are the most troublesome
> of all – idols which have crept into the understanding
> through the alliances of words and names. For men believe
> that their reason govern words; but it is also true that words
> react on the understanding; and this it is that has rendered
> philosophy and the sciences sophistical and inactive. [53]

iv. Idols of the Theatre (*Idola theatri*)

These are illusive knowledge obtained from the books we read and from the plays and movies we watch. These create in our minds a counterfeit world, a world of fantasy, and have the power to misguide our souls to perform acts that are either barbaric or not common among men. The dogmas of religion too falls under this category.

> But the *Idols of the Theatre* are not innate, nor do
> they steal into the understanding secretly, but are
> plainly impressed and received into the mind from
> the playbooks of philosophical systems and the
> perverted rules of demonstration.... *Idols of the*
> *Theatre* or *of Systems*, are many, and there can be
> and perhaps will be yet many more. For were it not
> that now for many ages men's minds have been

---

[53] Ibid., LIX.

busied with religion and theology; and were it not that civil governments, especially monarchies, have been averse to such novelties, even in matters speculative; so that men labor therein to the peril and harming of their fortunes – not only unrewarded, but exposed also to contempt and envy – doubtless there would have arisen many other philosophical sects like those which in great variety flourished once among the Greeks. For as on the phenomena of the heavens many hypotheses may be constructed, so likewise (and more also) many various dogmas may be set up and established on the phenomena of philosophy. [54]

5. Management Negligence

More good intentions, well-conceived programs, personal and organizational vitality, and potentially productive careers lie dead on the road because of poorly managed conflict and its potentially hideous consequences than due to any other ill facing organizations today – David Cowan. [55]

From a legal perspective, *negligence* is generally defined as *the*

---

[54] Francis Bacon, *The New Organon: The True Directions Concerning the Interpretations of Nature,* LXI-LXII.
[55] Cowan, 4.

failure to exercise reasonable care in a situation that causes harm to others or their property. [56] Note that *reasonable care* here is the yardstick that is used for justifying whether an action constitutes negligence or not. And this reasonable care we are talking about is case-specific; that is, it depends largely upon the exact circumstances that surround each case. This phenomenon is described in legal jargon as the "shifting sands" aspect of negligence, an issue legal practitioners often struggle with. [57] Also note that negligence can be either an *act* or *omission*. It is an act or omission when a tortfeasor or caregiver behaves unreasonably by doing a specific careless activity (*negligent* act) or by failing to do something that should have been done to prevent a disaster (*negligent omission*). [58]

Remember that in the very beginning, I began by highlighting the negligence of management in handling workplace conflicts as the major cause that so motivated me engage in this study. Rather than confronting workers' conflicts as they normally should, I have seen a number of managers, in an attempt to escape the complex demands involved in conflict resolution, turn a blind eye on workplace conflicts (*negligent omission*); others fearing it would be unethical if they sit back and do nothing after witnessing a conflict or after being informed of one wave their warning sword

---

[56] William R. Buckley and Cathy J. Okrent, *Torts & Personal Injury Law,* 3rd ed. (Canada: Thomson Delmar Learning, 2004), 18.
[57] Ibid., 18-19.
[58] Buckley and Okrent, 19.

to the conflicting parties, as football referees do to faulty players: *Next time in conflict, you both risk dismissal (negligent action)*. Can such a reaction from a manager actually stop the mouth of conflict from spilling its poisonous venom on its prey? Maybe it can to a certain extent. But what can we say of the action itself? Does it not constitute a threat, another type of conflict, one that weighs even heavier upon the shoulders of the conflicting parties than the prevailing issue itself? The manager's brutal reaction seems to validate John Burton's argument recorded in his publication entitled *Conflict Resolution as a Political System*. In this book, Burton argues that Western approaches to governance have been based on power rather than on the needs of the people being governed. [59]

Now looking at the other side of the coin, what about the performance or productivity of the workers at this juncture? Managers, as a strategy to avoid conflict resolution, often tend to ignore, back off, or intimidate workers to end conflict. They simply want the work environment to be calm. So, they use the threat of leadership power to enforce calmness. But does calmness in the atmosphere imply the absence of conflict? The real devil, unfortunately, that unsolicited tyrant that inflicts and restricts workers' productivity still remains. Or to pose our question in a

---

[59] Thomas Matyok, Jessica Seneyi and Sean Byrne, *Critical Issues in Peace and Conflict Studies: Theory, Practice, and Pedagogy* (USA: Rowman & Littlefield Education, 2011), 262.

different tone, do such managers understand fully the raison d'être for pursuing a resolution of conflict? Managers' outright negligence in handling workplace conflicts constitutes a great cost to an organization for conflicts have an inverse proportion to the organization's success - *the thesis of this project.*

4.6 Effects of Conflict in an Organization

1. Creates a Tensed and Unsafe Working Environment

> Most people go to work expecting to be able to carry out their workplace assignments in an atmosphere which is conducive to effective performance and which is psychologically and emotionally safe. Sadly, as the incidents of workplace bullying increase, so does the degree to which the workplace becomes an unsafe place for the people who are bullied and for those who observe what is happening and worry that they might be next in line. [60]

As conflict within an organization increases, so does the worker's insecurity. My experience as a business administrator seems to

---

[60] Aryanne Oade, *Managing Workplace Bullying: How to Identify, Respond to and Manage Bullying Behaviour in the Workplace* (UK: Palgrave Macmillan, 2009), 1.

reveal that a serene working atmosphere constitutes the most important factor that motivates workers' performance and their willingness to abide working for the organization in the foreseeable future. No matter how high an organization pays its workers, if the working environment of that organization is tensed, that is, if workers are at constant strives with one another due to management's inefficiency in designing the work to be done or negligence in handling workers' disputes, that organization will eventually suffer a massive loss; loss of productivity (due to the low performance of its workers), loss of manpower/talent (as disappointed, depressed, and heavy-hearted workers quit), and lastly loss of resources (as it engages more resources - moral, financial, technical, time - to recruit new talents).

It has occurred to me that most of the grievances of a few workers I have been privileged to listen to were focused hugely on interpersonal relationship issues (both vertical and horizontal) and work designs. Only a very few workers in developed countries have voiced concerns on financial issues (wages/ salaries/incentives). However, in the developing world, specifically in Cameroon where I headed a few posts of responsibility, both interpersonal relationship and irregularities in workers' financial motivation (incommensurate pay) seem to be on the stage, the latter being a sad story to write about.

2. Self-Isolation

The worker who has been criticized for a failed attempt to a task becomes even more cautious and reluctant to fully commit him/herself for fear of further criticism. As a course of action, the worker gradually isolates him/herself from the rest of the group. Such action, however, leads even to a further criticism by fellow coworkers. The former is accused of not communicating with others and lacking a spirit of collaboration. The bottom line is that the organization suffers a great loss due to the fraction of decreased commitment of the self-isolated worker.

3. Leads to Waste of Resources

> When we examine the negative results of poorly managed or unmanaged conflict, we see resources squandered on unproductive, if not counterproductive activities. On the other hand, when conflict is well managed and dealt with effectively, we not only conserve resources, we produce them. [61]

As will be discussed in Chapter 5, one of the results of a poorly arbitrated conflict is that it leaves the unsatisfied party wounded. As a result, the latter engages in actions that only undermine the success of the organization. Such actions may range from the willful commission of operation errors to the murder of a company staff (For a comprehensive reading, see *Violence* under *The*

---

[61] Cowan, 9.

Conflict Cycle in Chapter 5).

4. Loss of Trust in Management

As the body covers and protects the soul, so should the management of a corporation protect and guard their workers from any possible threat emanating from within or without the corporation.

> People who have been bullied, or who are currently being bullied, often feel betrayed by their employing organization. They find it inexcusable that senior managers who know about the issues they are facing can fail to confront the bullies and require them to stop using abusive behavior in the workplace. [62]

The trust workers have in management and the organization as a whole is very vital. Once this trust is gone, disorder and chaos will follow.

5. Can Precipitate/Cause Illness and Death

Conflict has a great potential of inciting psychological or physical pain on its victims, which may ultimately have grievous consequences. This claim I strongly believe is not hard to grasp especially if you are or have been a company employee and have been involved in a conflict situation. Concerning the above fact,

---

[62] Oade, 1.

Knapp & Daly write,

> Although conflict has the potential to increase understanding, stimulate positive change, and facilitate human relations, all too often conflict leads to intolerance and physical and psychological harm. The dysfunctional consequences of conflict are evident in terrorist activities and warfare between groups and nations, but they are not confined to interactions between members of such macroentities. [63]

Scientific facts reveal the following physical and psychological harm conflict imparts upon its victims: [64]

- In a ten-year study, individuals who could not manage their emotional stress had a 40% higher death rate than non-stressed individuals (p. 9).

- A Harvard Medical school study of 1,623 heart-attack survivors concluded that anger brought on by emotional conflicts doubled the risk of subsequent heart attacks compared to those who remained calm (p. 9).

---

[63] Mark L. Knapp & John A. Daly, eds., *Handbook of Interpersonal Communication (3rd ed.)* (USA: Sage Publications, Inc., 2002), 475.
[64] Don Colbert, *Deadly Emotions: Understand the Mind-Body-Spirit Connection that can Heal or Destroy You* (Nashville: Thomas Nelson, Inc., 2003), 9-10.

- A heart disease study at the Mayo Clinic found that psychological stress was the strongest predictor of future cardiac events, including cardiac death, cardiac arrest, and heart attack (p. 10).

7. Affects In-group Members and Creates Organizational Disorder

When you engage in a conflict with a man who is married and have children, you must bear in mind that any action of yours, no matter how justified it may be, is perceived by the man's family as an offence committed not only to their husband/father, but likewise to each family member.

> Conflict in an organization affects not only those who are directly involved, it also impacts those who are indirectly involved – the "innocent bystanders." Directly or indirectly, everyone connected with a conflict is affected at a personal level. [65]

In the organizational setting, there exist smaller social circles. Each circle is made up of workers who share some common qualities such as being from the same region or religion, or having same life ambitions. These qualities bring these people close together. When a group member suffers maltreatment of any sort, the others may react in a negative way to sympathize with their fellow member. In

---

[65] Cowan, 25.

2005, I witnessed a worker resign from a company two weeks after his friend was unjustly fired.

8. Others

Conflict has the following disadvantages to both the worker and organization: [66]

- Conflict may cause job stress, burnout, and dissatisfaction.

- Communication between individuals and groups may be reduced.

- Relationships may be damaged.

- A climate of distrust and suspicion can be developed.

- Job performance may be reduced.

- Organizational commitment and loyalty may be affected.

- Resistance to change can increase.

4.7 ADVANTAGES OF CONFLICTS

1. Draws Management's Attention

Conflict helps to uncover the weakness spots of management thereby drawing management's attention for a possible and quick action. When there is conflict, there is anger. Talking about anger,

---

[66] Rahim, 7.

Angela Zenteno-Hildago and Deanna Geddes assert, "Even as it is widely recognized to be associated with reduced employee well-being and decreased productivity, it also serves to help organizations and individuals to recognize and to adapt to problems and challenges."[67]

Conflict should not only draw management's attention but rather management should be prepared to tackle the problem from its root. To do so effectively, as we had earlier noted in our introduction, the organization must be endowed with emotional intelligence. Jochen I. Menges defines emotional intelligence as "the utilization of emotionally intelligent procedures, norms and behaviors throughout an organization"[68] in solving internal disputes. Menges further argues that "organizations can only realize their true productive potential through adoption of such intelligent procedures, norms, and behaviors."[69]

2. Conflict Prevents a System from being Stagnant

For Rahim, "Little or no conflict in organizations may lead to stagnation, poor decisions, and ineffectiveness."[70] However, Rahim acknowledged that conflicts left unattended may have dysfunctional consequences (Rahim, p. 12). Given Rahim's claim

---

[67] Neal. M. Ashkanasy, Charmine E.J. Hartel, and Wilfred J. Zerbe, eds., *Research on Emotion in Organizations (vol. 8): Experiencing and Managing Emotions in the Workplace* (UK: Emerald Group Publishing Ltd., 2012), 6.
[68] Ibid., 8.
[69] Ashkanasy, Hartel and Zerbe, 8.
[70] Rahim, 12.

that too little or too much conflict are both dysfunctional to an organization, Rahim & Bonoma (1979) further argue that a moderate amount of conflict handled in an appropriate manner is needed in an organization for its effectiveness. [71]

3. A Change Motivator

Another author with a positive outlook of conflict is Thomas Crum. Crum believes that the perception of conflict as dysfunctional is a myth. "Nature doesn't see conflict as negative," Crum argues. Rather, he continues, "Nature uses conflict as a primary motivator for change." [72]

Conflict may stimulate innovation, creativity, and growth (individuals and groups may be forced to search for new approaches). [73] Alternative solutions to a problem may be found.

4. An Educator of Others' Values

Conflict usually gives the disputing parties a unique opportunity to discuss and confront their differences. This confrontation enables both parties learn and appreciate each other's views, beliefs, and preferences, which goes a long way to strengthen their social ties and cooperation. [74] Theorists working at the dyadic level of

---

[71] Ibid.

[72] Thomas Crum, *The Magic of Conflict: Turning a Life of Work into a Work of Art* (USA: Touchstone, 1987), 6.

[73] Ibid., 7.

[74] William A. Donohue and Robert Colt, *Managing Interpersonal Conflict*

analysis have argued that emotional expressions help individuals know others' emotions, beliefs, and intentions, thus rapidly coordinating social interactions (Parrott, p. 178). Evidence shows communication of emotions conveys information about sender to receiver (Parrott, 178).

5. An Indicator of Management Inefficiency

The role that conflict plays in an organization is one that needs not to be overemphasized. By emerging, conflict seeks to be recognized and resolved. It is a phenomenon that must be addressed if the organization must function properly. Concerning the recognition of conflict, Pondy (1967: 504) argues that organization theories "that do not admit conflict provide poor guidance in dealing with problems of organizational efficiency, stability, governance, and change, for conflict within and between organizations is intimately related as either symptom, cause, or effect, to each of these problems. [75]

(California: Sage Publications Inc., 1992), 9.
[75] Rahim, 7.

CHAPTER 5

CONFLICT & MANAGEMENT INTERVENTION

5.1 The Conflict Cycle:

Potentiality →Covert →Overt →Wait & See →Violence

Conflict passes through five successive stages provided no management actions are taken upon awareness to prevent the conflict from further development. These stages, in progressive order, include: *Potentiality, Covert, Overt, Wait & See,* and *Violence.* In terms of reaction, violence is further divided into the 3F reaction modes that include: *Fold, Fight,* and *Flight.*

Stage 1 – Conflict Potentiality:

At this stage no identifiable conflict does exist. It kicks off when individuals and group members meet for the first time and begin familiarizing themselves with one another and with the demands of operations. This usually occurs during orientation phases of newly recruited staff or the orientation phase of a staff that has been transferred to a new department or office. Because interaction and communication at this level is usually shallow and superficial, individual preferences, values, beliefs, and goals are yet to be latched on. However, this first encounter gives both individuals an occasion to anticipate the identity of the other, which would shape the way they view and relate with each other in subsequent occasions. Thus a conflict potential is created when an individual so chooses to relate with the other in primitive ways, ways that are based on preconceptions. As an example, Michel, a young professional is posted to a company branch office. Upon arrival Michel discovers that the person he has to work with is a Muslim. With a preconceived notion of brutality held about Muslims, Michel feels frustrated. As an austerity measure, Michel ensures that some distance is always kept between him and his Muslim colleague. Even though the latter's character did not conform to Michel's preconception, the latter's faith posed a potential threat to Michel, thus creating a conflict potential in their work relationship. Another example to demonstrate conflict potentiality, a staff is awarded a $100 incentive for brilliant performance. This automatically creates a conflict potential between the staff in question and colleagues who were vying for the same incentive.

I experienced this form of conflict in 2004 working for a large multinational company based in Douala, Cameroon. This had to do with verbal incentive, not financial reward stated in the example above. In a management meeting of fifteen, my performance happened to have been commended by the Finance Manager, a commendation that inaugurated a conflict potential in my then Accounts Supervisor who was my immediate boss. The development of this conflict potential will be explained in their appropriate stages as we move further. For simplicity we shall label the Accounts Supervisor as *AS*.

Note that a conflict potential can turn into an intrapersonal conflict so long as the object of conflict remains unaware of the concern and the conflicted party ventures not to voice out such concern.

Stage 2 - Covert (Latent) Conflict:

> I begin to speak, but my lips deny passage to my words; A great force sends out my voice, and a greater holds it back. Heavenly gods, you can all witness that this thing that I desire, I do not desire.
>
> Seneca, *Phaedra*

At this stage, both parties become fully aware of their differences in goals, values, beliefs, and preferences. However, they refrain from verbal reactions since their differences pose no immediate threat to their respective positions. Either or both parties become embittered towards the other and try to humiliate the other through body languages. However, when their differences become unbearable, the conflict graduates to the overt stage. Note that most employees do not report conflicts due to the lack of an established system for conflict reporting in most organizations where workers can have the liberty to air out grievances. Another major problem is the rigidity of the hierarchy system. With the reporting lines being so tense, workers in fear of being penalized simply allow the embedded conflict to loiter within them, which as a parasite eats them up to a point where becoming helpless, they are forced to act.

Let us now demonstrate how the conflict potential in the AS developed into a covert conflict. Few days after the commendation exercise, I began experiencing a tense relationship with the AS, which led me to the recognition of a conflict. One day, he came and deposited on my desk five piles of documents to treat. One of these piles had to do with the accounting processing of Sales Waybills, documents whose processing I had not been taught by then. After finishing with the four piles, I called his office explaining I could not process the Sales Waybills, the reason being that I had not then received any training on them. He then asked me to bring them to his office. Upon arrival, he stretched forth his right hand in a bid to get hold of the documents, and said,

"I thought you were commended for hard work few days ago, you should have known how to process these documents by now. Okay, you can now go to your office; I will see what I can do." Now, coming to the full knowledge of this conflict reality, I became the more frustrated. How can I progress in a company where I have no good relationship with my boss who happens to be my direct evaluator? I kept wondering, and the conflict kept on escalating further.

Stage 3 - Overt (Manifest) Conflict:

At this level, conflict becomes perceivable by a third party as the conflicting parties, who can no longer hold themselves together, engage in public actions such as calling each other names. The intention of both parties is to bring their battle to the awareness of management for intervention.

The AS tried several plots to discredit me before the Finance Manager seeing that my rise in the company was imminent. He would avoid sending me to do jobs such as file sorting and file classification of expatriate documents that had to do with direct reporting to the Finance Manager.

Usually, before we leave the office at the close of work, we must inform the AS to ensure that we are not required to do any overtime (OT) work. One day, after finishing work, I did inform the AS I was leaving, and he gave me the go-ahead. In a taxi on my way home, my phone began ringing. That was the Finance

Manager (FM). He asked, "Mebinaji, where are you now?" I told him I was on my way home. He said, "Why did you leave without informing your supervisor? Don't you know there is OT?" I said to him, "I did, sir." He continued, "By the way, please come back to the office immediately." When I arrived the office, the FM had descended to the first floor where our department was located. He began a reiteration of the telephone interrogation, "Why did you leave without informing your supervisor? When I reemphasized that I did and the AS gave his approval, the AS declined the allegation. Fortunately enough, a chief of staff for Shipment, who overhead the AS giving me the go-ahead to leave, intervened. That is how I was rescued before the FM. But the struggle continued since no attempt was made by the FM who by then should have known something was not right.

Stage 4 - Wait & See Conflict:

After having engaged in a public display, both parties temporarily withdraw their provocative actions. This time they are simply waiting to be called in by a hierarchy for a formal investigation and resolution of conflict. Most managers tend to consider this state as a phenomenon whereby parties themselves ended up resolving their disputes through the act of confrontation; and thus ignored a formal investigation altogether. Realizing that no such intervention is forthcoming or possible, parties cast the die to engage in violence.

This stage marks a transition period of conflict – from *manifest* to *violence*. As the Wait & See stage comes to a close, conflict evolves to a brutish, ungovernable, and insuppressible state, a state that could be likened to a bloody civil war between two nations that had failed to come to the negotiating table.

After much trouble with the AS, and with the scene that happened to have humiliated the AS before the FM, I waited dispassionately expecting to be called by the FM for interrogation to no avail. With no such call forthcoming, I finally took a "violent" decision. See continuation below.

Stage 5 - Violence

> The most terrible consequence of interpersonal conflict is violence. When people do not have the skills to resolve conflicts, they automatically resort to whatever methods they've learned, often choosing aggression or complete withdrawal – David Cowan. [76]

As stated above, conflict at this stage becomes very difficult to handle. The conflicting individual here is hardly opened to dialogue. His/her singular goal now is to carry out his/her intended action depending on which mode of reaction he/she chooses: fold, fight, or flight.

---

[76] Cowan, 28.

Violence Mode 1 - Fold:

The person engages in counter-productive behaviors as a measure to retaliate to the organization's passiveness to respond to issues he considers considerably significant. Such counter-productive behaviors include intentional errors and time wastage on operations, misuse and theft of company properties, hostility towards fellow workers, backstabbing, to name a few. Note that the individual here has no clear intention to leave the company, but wishes to appease his frustrations and anger by engaging in such conducts.

Violence Mode 2 - Fight

When we hear about violent acts in the workplace, we often think of the perpetrators as strange or evil people. They are not. For the most part they are just average people who lost control of situations that could have been managed – David Cowan. [77]

We all have heard some of the most horrible stories that occur within company walls: An employee threatening to deal with a supervisor for an appraisal bias that stops him from progressing onto a higher rung of the company's ladder of hierarchy; a disgruntled staff deliberately ignoring the orders of a manager as a protest for the latter's inappropriate conduct; an employee vowing

---

[77] Cowan, 28.

to murder his boss for racial discrimination, just to name these few. Workplace violence constitutes a real threat to business success. According to Workplace Violence Research Institute, workplace violence costs businesses in the U.S. more than $36 billion each year. [78]

The good news is that workplace violence can be averted. This is because although a few of them may come out of the blue, that is, with no warning, a significant proportion is preceded by verbal bullying and threats, which when properly investigated would lead the way for the surgery of the violence or conflict in question. An immediate investigative action of violence is an important management policy for an organization. It sends a clear message to the entire staff body: *Here, violence not welcome.* Because most violence usually escalate from verbal aggression to the use of physical weapons, they must be stopped at their earliest stage of awareness. If not, the organization must be prepared to deal with a much bigger problem - property damage or staff loss.

It is worthy to note that workplace violence is not only perpetrated by insiders, it is a result of outsiders as well. For example, a gang robbing a bank; a romantic lover or family member targeting an employee for murder. In fact Attorney Lisa Guerin argues that contrary to popular belief, a major proportion of violence in the workplace is caused by outsiders. [79] Notwithstanding, this project

---

[78] Lisa Guerin, *The Essential Guide to Workplace Investigations* (USA: Nolo, 1964), 268.

focuses exclusively on conflicts perpetrated by insiders to insiders. So all of our attention will be directed to this regard.

Because an organization legally bears the liability of workplace violence for which it failed to take preventive measures [80], the organization must do all it can to handle violence accordingly. Under the Occupational Safety and Health Act (OSH Act), the employer must provide the employee with a workplace that is free of any recognizable hazard likely to cause the employee harm or death. [81] The Occupational Safety and Health Administration enforcing the OSH Act has recently reclassified workplace violence to constitute a hazard. [82]

Violence Mode 3 - Flight

In order to avoid the problem for good, the person decides to quit the organization altogether. To continue our conflict example, I finally made a decision to resign from the company after having negotiated for a job in another company. All efforts by the FM to reverse my decision failed. I was so embittered not just with the AS but with the entire organization for their outright negligence.

---

[79] Ibid., 269.
[80] Guerin, 277.
[81] Ibid.
[82] Ibid,, 277-278.

5.2 The Lifecycle of a Conflicted Worker

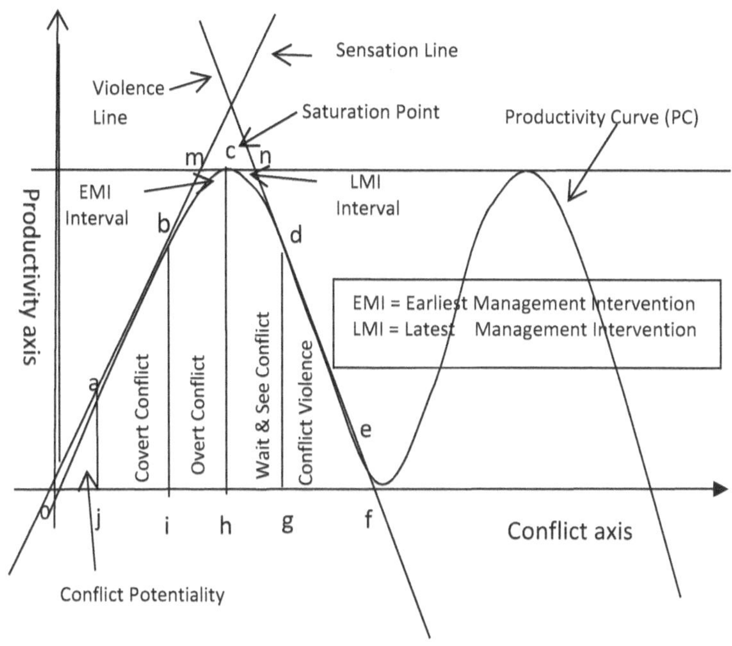

In the figure above, the point 0 represents the origin. At this point, conflict is zero. It represents the point where the worker is recruited by the organization. However, as the new recruit begins his/her first day of work, he/she begins to discern interpersonal differences with other workers. The worker has just entered the stage of conflict we referred to above as *conflict potentiality* stage. Here, the worker identifies potential factors within the organization, its system, and people that have some default characteristics in them to generate conflicts.

As the Productivity Curve (PC) touches the Sensation Line (at point a), the worker begins to perceive the existence of conflict. He can now tangibly identify conflict elements within the system and with fellow colleagues as work goes on. This marks the beginning of the *covert* (or latent) *conflict* stage. The worker suffers a great victimization from the workers of the organization (manager, supervisor, coworkers) but chooses to remain nonvocal for they fear a retaliation may have a boomerang effect.

However, as the victimization tarries, the affected worker prepares for reaction. The PC begins to depart from the Sensation Line (at point b) towards the Violence Line. The worker now engages in a physical confrontation with their persecutor, which we will refer to as *conflict actor* (the affected worker who receives the conflict being the *conflict reactor*). This stage of conflict is referred to as the *overt* (or manifest) *conflict* stage.

As the physical confrontation continues, the worker becomes increasingly depressed to a point where their productivity can no longer improve as the worker's capability to produce is completely overshadowed by the prevailing circumstances. This is the *saturation point* (point c). It is the point at which productivity reaches its maximum level. It occurs when the Sensation and Violence lines do intersect. The worker at this point is in a total dilemma: Tell management and wait, or engage in violence? The worker, in a limited number of cases, decides to keep management informed (or, in most cases, assumes management is/should be aware) and wait for a quick management intervention. This stage we refer to as the *wait & see* stage.

After waiting for a period, and realizing no solution is forthcoming, the worker begins to act violently as we had described above under the 3F Reaction modes of violence (Fold - Fight - Flight).

Note that triangle bmc represents the interval at which the intervention of management is needed as earliest as possible as conflicted workers begin engaging in a physical confrontation. Triangle cnd, on the other hand, denotes the latest time interval management must act if it is to avoid any escalation of violence and regain organizational output.

5.3 What You Need to Effectively Resolve a Conflict

1. Solid Vision and Optimism

In the famous story of the three bricklayers working side by side, each of them is asked, "What are you doing?" One replies, "I am laying bricks." The second replies, "I am constructing a wall," but the third answered, "I am building a cathedral." While the first two had a narrow scope by limiting their vision, the third carried the vision all along. While the other men were process-oriented, the third was goal-oriented. While they saw the building of a cathedral as an ambiguous task, the third saw the building process already completed in the construction of the wall.

The same applies with managers who launch enquiries to resolving conflicts faced by employees. Some managers may boycott the resolution process during the investigation stage after discovering the complexity of the conflict. To account to a higher hierarchy, they come up with measures that do not deal with the root cause of the problem. Such managers are short-sighted. They are intimidated by seeing the complex building plan of the cathedral. Because they lack the motivation to visualize the finished structure of the cathedral, they quit.

When asked about the challenges he faces in managing organizational crisis, Mark Swilling, co-director of the Sustainability Institute said, "The leadership challenge, from our point of view, is not to get discouraged by the logic of the existing system. The leadership challenge that excites me is to inspire the system to change." [83] Where there is no change in employee attitude and, hence, output, conflict prevails. A true resolution of conflict brings genuine system change: restores order and performance.

2. Empathy:

A well-known American is known to have said, "We should not judge another person until we have walked two moons in his moccasins." The implication here is that we should always try to

---

[83] Gerzon, 219.

envisage or imagine how a person in conflict feels before we can make any judgment. In other words, we should walk in the moccasins of the conflicted for a while as this would enable us reach an objective judgment of facts.

Empathy, as defined by Avery, is "the ability to recognize and understand another person's perceptions and feelings, and to accurately convey that understanding through an accepting response." [84] Defining empathy from a cultural perspective, Ting-Toomey writes, "Through empathy we are willing to imaginatively place ourselves in the dissimilar other's cultural world and to experience what she or he is experiencing" (Samovar et al., 2010: 389). As important as cultural values are, we must stress that more emphasis must be placed on the psychological state of the conflicted. To this, Miller & Steinberg remark, "To communicate interpersonally, one must leave the cultural and sociological levels of predications and physically travel to the psychological level" (Samovar et al., 2010: 389).

Note that empathy is a complex activity composed of many variables as described here by Bell:

> Cognitively, the empathic person takes the perspective of another person, and in so doing strives to see the world from the other's point of

---

view. Affectively, the empathic person experiences the emotions of another; he or she feels the other's experiences. Communicatively, the empathic individual signals understanding and concern through verbal and nonverbal cues. [85]

In one of the organizations I had worked before, a case was reported to our branch manager. This related to sexual assault committed by a counselor to my then fiancée who had been sent to the accused for counseling services. During investigation, it was discovered that the accused, knowing his wife had travelled, did invite the victim to his house where he assaulted her. After the claim was discovered to be true, the manager, as a way of solving the crisis, called me into his office and apologized for what went wrong, and said, "Please, don't let people know about this for it will spoil our reputation." Yet no sanction was given to the counselor. The same man marched into his office the next day conducting business as usual. He would even come to my office (Accounting & Finance) boldly making cash requests. I felt frustrated, intimidated, marginalized, battered, and tattered. For me, business was not as usual. I lost every motivation I had for work. I could barely balance the books of accounts. My input consistently went down and down until I decided to quit in the third month after finding a job in another company.

---

[85] Samovar et al., 389.

3. Know Well to Lead Well

Why is *understanding the plight and values of your workers* so important in leadership and conflict management in particular? A great leader, to borrow Hitler's words, is a *Menschenkenner*. That is, "one who grasps - instinctively, intuitively or otherwise - the motives of men." [86]

Over the past 2000 years, emotions have been viewed to occupy a central role in organizational management (Mastenbrock, 2000). Fayol, for example, stressed that leaders should understand so well all aspects of their workers' psyches including their emotional states. [87]

The psychology of a man reveals the veritable mental disposition of that man at any given point in time, context, and under any given situation. With regards to work, an employee's psyche is the *mental duplex* of that employee, which has been gradually built over the entire period of employment with either the disappointments, achievements, or a mélange of both, which the employee has harbored since their inception and involvement in the affairs of the organization. You cannot predict the type of upholstery in your neighbor's house unless you actually visit your neighbor and see for yourself what furniture they have. Comments

---

[86] Hodgkinson, 67.
[87] Bryman et al., 365.

and suggestions are only possible after a physical confrontation with reality. In the same way, for a leader to be a good shepherd, councilor, motivator, and liberator of workers in conflict, the leader must from time to time engage in casual and deep conversations with workers to know who they really are and what they like or dislike about work and the organization as a whole.

Brief, what we are saying here is that leaders must be able to understand the emotions of their subordinates, irrespective of the latter's attempt to suppress or conceal them from view. Knowing to some extent the different cultures of your workers and how they express emotions in their respective cultures would be helpful since emotional expression varies with cultures. Understanding cultural parameters, like facial expressions, gestures, tone of voice, moods, etc., that are used in expressing frustrations in the workplace would be very critical in launching a formal investigation that seeks to eliminate the problem so that the worker can be emotionally liberated for maximum productivity.

Note that by saying leaders understand the psyches of their workers, we are not saying that leaders must be able to determine the precise readings on the chemical and mental thermometers of the said workers at every given point in time. Rather, what we are saying is that leaders should, at least, be able to predict this reading through their experiences of interactions with workers.

4. Effective Communication

Communication is defined by Lehman & Dufrene as "the process of exchanging information and meaning between or among individuals through a common system of symbols, signs, and behavior." [88] Good communication skills on the part of the negotiator are vital ingredients for resolving conflicts. They require that the negotiator be attentive and observant as parties talk, making inferences from and responding logically to parties' arguments. Effective communication does to the soul what medicine does to the body. It heals a broken soul, relieves it from pressure, and re-conditions it to a "new state" through the mechanism of persuasion.

Charles Darwin & the Principles of Expression

On the importance of understanding the principles of expression, Charles Darwin in *The Principle of Antithesis* developed in *The Expression of the Emotions in Man and Animals,* considered one of his most scholarly works, writes:

> With social animals, the power of intercommunication between the members of the same community, - and with other species, between the opposite sexes, as well as between

---

[88] Carol M. Lehman and Debbie D. Dufrene, *Business Communication,* 16th ed. (USA: Cengage Learning, 2010), 4.

the young and the old, - is of the highest importance to them. This is generally affected by means of the voice, but it is certain that gestures and expressions are to a certain extent mutually intelligible. Man not only uses inarticulate cries, gestures, and expressions, but has invented articulate language; if, indeed, the word INVENTED can be applied to a process, completed by innumerable steps, half-consciously made. Anyone who has watched monkeys will not doubt that they perfectly understand each other's gestures and expression, and to a large extent, as Rengger asserts, those of man. [89]

5.4 RESOLVING WORKPLACE CONFLICTS

Given its importance to personal and organizational wellbeing, the issue of conflict management should never be carelessly dismissed. Taking for granted that the average person can manage conflict, even passably, involves assumptions that individuals and organizations can no longer afford to make. [90]

---

[89] Charles Darwin, *The Expression of the Emotions in Man and Animals* (Teddington: The Echo Library, 2007), 30.

> If we want more peace, we must have less conflict - be in conflict less of the time, which is not to say eliminate conflict, but is to say manage and resolve it better – David Cowan [91]

Conflict resolution is a managerial activity that must be given proper attention. It must neither be postponed nor ignored. Conflict resolution must be timely, appropriate, and unbiased. No one resolution method applies to all conflicts. The method to be applied to resolve or eliminate a conflict depends largely upon the nature of the conflict in question – the source and duration of conflict, relationship and parties' attitudes towards conflict, disgruntlements, priorities and needs of conflicted parties, etc. Note that not all resolved conflicts have the same results. The quality of change that is experienced by disputants following a conflict resolution depends largely on the skills employed in the resolution process to bring about such change.

Also note that,

> A workable rule of thumb holds that the consequences of an unmanaged or poorly managed conflict are disproportionately larger than the conflict itself. We should keep this rule in mind when we are tempted to dismiss a conflict because we don't think

---

[90] Cowan, 7.
[91] Ibid., 3.

it requires our attention. Nowhere in life is the adage "an ounce of prevention is worth a pound of cure" more applicable than in the realm of conflict – David Cowan. [92]

Conflict Resolution Procedures

Here is a procedure that should be observed in resolving conflicts skillfully and in a way that leaves conflicting parties unhurt and fulfilled.

- Talk privately with each conflicting party to have their side of the story. As the party discusses, make sure you listen attentively and take notes. Note that the intention of the speaker is to be heard, to be understood, and to be attended to. Also note that no judgment should be based on a one-sided story. The intention here is to have a full knowledge of what led to the conflict – putting the two separate views together. Note that in cases of conflicts involving a leader and a direct subordinate or conflicts between staff of unequal administrative hierarchy, one party, usually the subordinate or lower-ranked staff, may avoid making certain confessions that may damage the reputation of the

---

[92]Cowan, 29.

leader or hierarchy. Such a worker feels unsaved to speak up against and in the presence of his boss. In such a situation, memo previously taken from the one-to-one talk could guide the negotiator. At this juncture, the negotiator, a senior hierarchy, can remind and request the employee to reecho any omitted claims.

- Invite both parties for dialogue.

- Acknowledge a difficult situation exists.

- Acknowledge both parties have some reasons for being offended. Let them know that in most cases of conflicts, neither party is right nor wrong; rather, parties' distinctive perceptions collide to form an array of disagreement.

- Share a cup of drink together with both parties to diffuse anger.

- Share a conflict experience or story to enable parties know that conflicts are quite a natural phenomenon.

- Listen effectively to both parties as they share their story. Effective listening demands that the listener be calm, dispassionate, and sincere. Make sure you understand so well what each party is saying. If not ask questions, focusing on the party's side of the story. Being passionate can send a bad message to the other party that you are being subjective or biased, which may hamper the whole process of negotiation.

- Establish a common area of agreement, no matter how small, and complement both parties for this.

- Define the area of disagreement.

- Take action to resolve disagreement: This is the level that requires enough application of brainpower after a careful and objective analysis of the conflict situation. The quality of decision taken would determine the degree of liberation to be experienced by conflicted parties, which will ultimately determine parties' levels of commitment to the organizational goal. The negotiator <u>must</u> be careful to avoid slanting for whatsoever reasons. Some possible actions may include: modifying the nature of staff interdependence (rotate or exchange staff), reconsidering the reporting chain, increasing management supervision, etc.

- Determine what to do such as bringing in a higher hierarchy or an outside expert for mediation if conflict remains unresolved.

5.5 BENEFITS OF CONFLICT RESOLUTION

1. High Productivity

This being the case, it appears that in the

> management of conflict a wonderful opportunity
> exists to enhance effectiveness and productivity
> while deepening commitment to the human side of
> the organization – David Cowan. [93]

Resolving or eliminating a workplace conflict involving an employee helps restore the employee's mental soundness, which gives the employee the optimum chance to improve the value of services rendered to customers and stakeholders in general. The better the satisfaction derived from resolved conflicts, the better the quality of services to be rendered to customers. As will be shown shortly in the next chapter (Conflict & Productivity), conflict does hinder the productivity of the worker. If you had visited a few companies in the past, you could tell from the caliber of services you received which amongst those companies' workers had a few unresolved work issues.

In June 2012, I made a short trip to Cameroon to visit family members. In front of the cash desk of a small bank, three of us were lining up for withdrawals. When the first on the line, an old man with an emergency case, beckoned on the bank staff who seemed to have been very slow, to speed up the service, the old man was rather responded to harshly: "Don't you see I'm working? Please, hold on!" Irritated, I cautioned the bank official: "Sir, is that the way you respond to customers? Do you think that's

---

[93] Cowan, 4.

professional?" And I was met with even harsher words: "I don't care! Are you the one to teach me my job?" Annoyed the more, I immediately left for a nearby branch where I was served with dignity. Same bank with supposedly same rules across its branches; but while the service rendered by one branch was tensed, that rendered by the other was amicable. Clearly, there was some personal conflict of interest going on with the gloomy bank official that had not been duly taken care of.

Any business that must survive must be able to sustain the satisfaction level of its clients by improving or at least maintaining the expected product/service quality, a process which can only be achieved by truly liberated workers. Note that a slight drop in the satisfaction of a client can cause an enormous drop in the loyalty of that client, and hence an enormous drop in sales. And losing a client because of product/service quality issues is even worse. This is because losing a client means losing all the potential streams of purchases to be realized from that single client.

2. Prevents Disruption of Operations

Conflicts can be a great cost to an organization as they are capable of slowing down or halting business operations, which are simply a chain of activities. The conflict, for example, arising from the Sales department can have enormous consequences on the Accounting department that requires source documents relating to sales in order to draw up financial records. Thus, liberating the worker is necessary if he/she must continue on operations.

3. Enforcement of policies

It helps enforce company policies to prevent further misconducts. When workers do realize the company has strengthened its policies, everyone would become more cautious of their actions.

4. Vertical Reporting

It fosters or encourages vertical reporting. Investigating conflict matters encourages employees to report or come forward with workplace clashes.

5. Employee Loyalty

It gives employees a good impression about their organization. When employees realize that management has much interest in addressing and putting an end to matters that relate to them, they become more loyal to the organization.

6. Prevents Lawsuits

It prevents the organization against lawsuits on account of negligence in investigating workplace conflicts that resulted to violence. [94] The following example would shed more light on this:

Ralph was accused of sexually harassing two female coworkers.

---

[94] Guerin, 6.

After the company carried out a thorough investigation, interviewing the two victims, Ralph, and five others whom Ralph suggested, the company found out that Ralph had sexually harassed the victims. Ralph was then fired.

Ralph later sued the company under the pretext that he had a consensual affair with both victims and that they were only angry with him for two-timing them, claiming there was no sexual harassment. Ralph accused the company of unjust termination demanding damages. However, an appeals court ruled that because the company carried out a fair and thorough investigation and reached a good-faith conclusion based on the evidence available, the company was not liable for firing Ralph. [95]

5.6 HOW TO PREVENT WORKPLACE CONFLICTS

1. Educate & Value Workers

A proper organizational training and attention accorded to employees' welfare has numerous advantages to an organization. While a comprehensive training prepares employees on handling business operations, company education prepares them to effectively handle a broad range of issues that are vital for the company's existence. This may include personnel matters such as company standards for inter-relationships (e.g. ethics, conduct,

---

[95] Guerin, 7.

communication, beliefs, etc.). Concerning the role of education, Vaclav Havel, the former president of the Republic of Czech affirmed, "Education is the ability to perceive the hidden connections between phenomena." [96] The education that workers acquire from their organization enables them make better decisions regarding work operations and the motives of their fellow coworkers without which the birth of conflict would have been a recurrent process within the work process.

Thorough staff training also helps in reducing the amount of management supervision on employees and fosters mastery of operations leading to a more efficient and increased productivity.

> The future of your organization and the potential of your employees are intertwined; their destinies are linked. An organization can only become the-best-version-of-itself to the extent that the people who drive that organization are striving to become better-versions-of-themselves. [97]

And when both the employee and the organization are falling short of becoming better-versions-of-themselves for the achievement of organizational goal (due to inadequate employee training and supervision), a career conflict is born – while the organization accuses the employee of incompetence, the latter accuses the

---

[96] Gerzon, 31.
[97] Matthew Kelly, *The Dream Manager* (USA: Beacon Publishing, 2007), 1.

former of not providing adequate training and supervision that would enable him/her better handle the job. At the level of the organization, the conflict can be resolved by providing the employee with further training. But when the organization chooses not to do so, it creates in the employee what Ashkanasy (2003a) identifies as "emotion at the within-person level." [98] This emotion shapes the attitude of the worker, which leads to judgment-driven behavior such as quit or engage in counter-productive behavior.

2. Develop Workers' Career

If there is one thing that every worker in an organization aspires for, one thing that every person duly employed in a business venture truly yearns for, that one thing is *career development*. No one wants to remain at the same level of expertise, organizational knowledge, and performance throughout the foreseeable duration of their commitment. Over the past thirty years, as an increasing number of workers devolve or throw away the idea of staying with the same company for their entire careers, many companies are seeking ways of inspiring and retaining such workers. [99] Giving workers opportunities to develop their talents to be more instrumental to the organization may just be the answer. With the geometrical decrease of skilled labour in the job market, workers

---

[98] Bryman et al., *The SAGE Handbook of Leadership*, 366.
[99] Kelly, ix.

generally (and naturally) hunger for a successive development of their careers over time to enable them better handle the company's growing and complex work demands. Another major reason why workers are longing for their career development is that such a professional progress would constitute a collateral security for their retention in the company books.

Concerning the retention of workers, let us listen to what Patrick Lencioni, author of *The Five Dysfunctions of a Team,* has to say:

> Executives today realize that the cost of losing good people is no longer limited to higher recruiting and retraining expenses; it is a recipe for failure. Even the most cynical manager will admit that one of the most important competitive advantages a company can have is the ability to keep and motivate the human capital that is in such short supply... But when it comes to inspiring people and creating the kind of environment where employees laugh at the notion of leaving their company, there is something far more powerful – and less expensive – that companies have largely overlooked. [100]

As Matthew Kelly points out, a greater proportion of company workers today are *actively disengaged,* [101] a disengagement that

---

[100] Kelly, x.

[101] Ibid., 1.

costs companies huge sums of money in their payrolls. According to *Business Week* reports (2007), 21% of top management jobs and 24% of all management jobs irrespective of function, region, and industry will become vacant by 2017. [102]

Most companies across the globe have put in place a concrete structure for the recruitment of workers, a structure that enables them pull out of the job market the most talented candidates for employment. However, what a number of them have not been able to do is providing enough professional encouragement to their employees as the latter engage in the business of the organization. Thus, the recruiting company must seek ways of improving the career of its workers for, as Kelly notes, it is not just enough to recruit talent, but attracting, engaging, and retaining such talent should form the primary strategic objective of every successful modern organization. [103]

3. Create an Ethical Workplace

> Why is business ethics important? A keen and in-depth understanding of business ethics is important to the long-run viability of a corporation. A thorough knowledge of business ethics is also important to the well-being of the individual officers

---

[102] Ibid., 2.
[103] Kelly, 3.

and directors of the corporation, as well as to the welfare of the firm's employees. [104]

One of the main reasons why conflicts occur in a geometric fashion in most organizations today is due to the lack of ethical standards and/or their applicability in the workplace. When ethical standards are no longer an issue of corporate concern, workers take good advantage of this to operate as they so wish – assigning coworkers, especially new and inexperienced ones, and requesting them for favors without any iota of courtesy and respect.

The Affective Events Theory (Weiss & Cropanzano, 1996), has shown that the behavior and performance of a worker are determined by the worker's experiences at work, and not so much by interpersonal differences such as personality (Fisher, 2000). [105] This theory suggests that affect varies over time and is influenced by factors such as mood cycles and other factors within the work environment. These factors largely influence the way workers react to workplace events (Ashton-James & Ashkanasy, 2005). [106]

I stood by Maheji and watched a coworker, Raul, pushing and unleashing a platform trolley towards Maheji expecting the latter would bring the trolley to a halt and park it where it ought to. A

---

[104] Roger LeRoy Miller and William Eric Hollowell, *Business Law: Text & Exercises, 6th ed.* (USA: Cengage Learning, 2011), 15.
[105] Ashkanasy, Hartel, and Zerbe, *Research on Emotion in Organizations*, 14.
[106] Ibid.

single word in Japanese, お願いします, for *"Please, do me this favor,"* would have sufficed. Yet, not only did Raul not offer this word of politeness, his attitude was far from communicating politeness. As soon as he unleashed the trolley towards Maheji, Raul turned away from Maheji. Embittered, Maheji turned to me and in a low voice said, 何それ, meaning, "What's the meaning of that!" After saying this, he then caught the trolley and had it parked. Such events had occurred a number of times within this department and even at the view of some of its leaders to an extent that they have somehow become a custom to some. What we can say here is that the leadership of this department has failed woefully in instituting the right ethical environment for work operations. A leader or manager of a department or organization is the referee of morality, values, and standards of the people who are subject to their supervision. What the leader says, does not say, does, does not do, matters so much in building a strong, conflict-free workplace as surveys of business executives have revealed that employees predetermine their next course of action from their manager's attitude. [107]

4. Design a Public Space for Dialogue

Workplace relationships are usually very formal and tensed. My little experience is that a majority of company employees do not know who their colleagues really are because they have not taken

---

[107] Miller and Hollowell, 15.

adequate time together for a deep informal fellowship. Public spaces provide workers with a unique opportunity to know one another deeply through the medium of casual dialogue. As workers meet and talk about personal issues, they gain one another's trust, and, as a result, exercise caution and patience when dealing with the other during work operations. Such an occasion strengthens ties, fosters co-operation, and thus serves as a motivating drive for both parties in derogating or annulling any potential conflict of interest.

5. Create an Open Communication System

> Although many companies have openness as one of
> their corporate values, few are adept at translating it
> into practical processes and instinctive behaviour. [108]

An open communication system benefits the business in many ways. It helps workers "overcome hidden fears" [109] such as: "Do they really accept me as part of the organization?" "Are they hiding certain information from me?" "Do they perceive me in the organization as I perceive myself?" With an open communication system, workers are very much open to speak up and air out issues of concerns. This, Clutterbuck & Hirst write, "reduces the build-up of hidden resistance and ensures that the feedback top management

---

[108] David Clutterbuck and Sheila Hirst, *Talking Business: Making Communication Work* (UK: The Item Group Ltd., 2002), 101.
[109] Ibid., 102.

receives is more genuine and accurate." [110]

---

[110] Ibid.

CHAPTER 6

THE CASE STUDY

T he case study method is one of several methods of conducting research in the social sciences. Other ways or methods may include surveys, experiments, histories, and economic and epidemiologic research. [111]

6.1 What is a Case Study?

Before we get into this definition, it will be worthwhile to define what a *case* is, a word whose meaning we often assume in our everyday usage. However, we may be dumbfounded when requested to state its literal meaning. Let us look at this comprehensive definition given to us by Bill Gillham. Gillham

---

[111] Robert K. Yin, *Case Study Research: Design and Methods, 4th ed.* (USA: SAGE Publications Inc., 2009), 2.

defines a case as "a unit of human activity embedded in the real world; which can only be studied or understood in context; which exists in the here and now; that merges in with its context so that precise boundaries are difficult to draw." [112] A case could be an individual, a group of individuals, an organization, or a process. In simple terms, we could say a case study is a conscious endeavor to investigate the above in order to come up with answers to our research questions.

For the sake of depth, here are other definitions of case study. According to Schramm (1971), case studies are "inquiries that try to illuminate a decision or set of decisions: why they were taken, how they were implemented and with what results." For Mitchell (1983), a case study is "a detailed examination of an event (or a series of related events) that the analyst believes exhibits the operation of some identified general theoretical principles." Yin (1994) defines a case study research as "an empirical inquiry that investigates a contemporary phenomenon within its real-life context; when the boundaries between phenomenon and context are not clearly evident and in which, multiple sources of evidence are used." All three quotations are obtained from Taylor et al., 2006: 25. Thus, Taylor et al. write, the definition for a case study could be summarized as "an intensive, detailed description and analysis of a particular individual, group or event." The main

---

[112] Bill Gillham, *Case Study Research Methods* (London: Continuum, 2000), 1.

sources of information for a case study include physical observation, interviews, and archival records (Taylor et al., 2006: 25).

Case studies favor a detailed analysis of contextual factors that affect events in the case under scrutiny. Rather than using a large sample size and following a rigid protocol to establish a case, a case study involves "an in-depth, longitudinal examination of a single instance or event" (Taylor et al., 2006: 25).

6.2 When Should We Use a Case Study?

An important question to ask is, "When should we use the case study as a method for conducting research? The case study method should be used, Yin stresses, when a research meets the following conditions: [113]

a) Research questions pose questions relating to 'how' and 'why'. Questions of this caliber require more explanations as they attempt to address events that are associated with human behavior and organizational functions in general, which can only be properly accessed over a period of time through the study of a case or cases (Yin, 2009: 9).

b) The investigator has little or no control over events (that is, variables) that make up the research.

---

[113] Yin, 2.

c) The research addresses contemporary issues in a real-life context as opposed to historical issues. This condition largely distinguishes case study researches from other forms of research (Yin, 2009: 2).

Due to the richness of evidence and broadness of the real-life situation, a case study would provide much more variables of interest, which had not been previously forecasted, than mere data points (Yin, 2009: 2). As a result, an important technique in undergoing a case study research, Yin suggests, is to collect evidence from all available sources with data from the respective sources converging "in a triangulating fashion." [114]

6.5 THE CASE STUDY PROPER

1. Approach

For the purpose of this research, a qualitative design from a phenomenological approach was used. This approach allows best to capture emotion experiences (Sandberg, 2000). [115] According to Sandberg, this form of research is simply an interpretation of the person's lived experiences. And these experiences, Sandberg continues, are simply a product of the individual's personality and their place of abode, in this case the work environment. Although there exist some negative viewpoints concerning the qualitative

---

[114] Yin, 2.
[115] Ashkanasy, Hartel, and Zerbe, 19.

approach, Woods and Catanzaro (1988) argue that the validity of a qualitative research accounts for one of its biggest advantages. [116]

2. Objective

The objective of this case study was to capture and analyze the experiences and feelings of workers during times of conflict in a typical work setting. It is also designed to evaluate the impact conflict has on both the worker's productivity and on the overall organizational stability. Last, but not the least, the project is designed to investigate how workers cope with this social malaise we refer to as conflict.

3. Participants

The case study consisted of five participants from four different nationalities: Japan (2), Peru (1), Bangladesh (1), and Cameroon (1). Participants were all workers of a glass screen engineering company based in the Saitama prefecture of Japan, which is situated in the north of Tokyo. For simplicity, the Case Study Participants shall be referred to as CSPs.

4. Criteria for Inclusion

The first criterion for consideration of potential CSPs was the language of research (English or Japanese). Only workers who

---

[116] Ashkanasy, Hartel, and Zerbe, 19.

could speak either English or Japanese were considered as potential CSPs. The second criterion included the willingness to participate. Among the potential CSPs, only those who were willing to participate in the research process and were willing to be granted an interview were selected as CSPs. Apart from these two criteria, no effort was made to control gender, age, race, academic qualifications, work experience and hierarchy.

5. Sampling Method and Procedure

Questionnaires relating to the subject of research were distributed out to fifteen workers. The objective was to sample a variety of views from workers. Out of this number, eleven questionnaires were returned making a response rate of 73%. Out of the eleven questionnaires, five candidates were selected to constitute the CSPs.

In addition to the selection criteria we have just stated above, the researcher carefully selected from the list of returned questionnaires, employees who work in the manufacturing department. This was because the researcher happened to have been a worker in this department. It gave me the possibility to witness and follow up the research with the CSPs with limited time. Fortunately, this department seemed to be the most conflict-prevalent in the entire company. In the manufacturing department, work is done 24 hours a day (in two shifts). The nature of work is such that workers must cooperate for the final production to be realized. Work is done in a chain process. This work process of interdependence made the occurrence of interpersonal (and other forms of) conflicts very likely within this department.

CSPs were predominantly male (four in number, making 80%). One of them was a female (making only 20%). Two of the CSPs were between the ages of 25 and 35, while the other three were between the ages of 35 and 45. Two of them have been working in the same industry for 0 to 3 years. The other three have been working in the same industry for 4 to 8 years

6. Data Collection

The trustworthiness of this research and the data collected is an important aspect to be considered. Before and after interviews were conducted, the researcher had observed the CSPs (job shadowing) for close to six months as they carried out their daily work activities. Observation notes were taken on the spot in each of these exercises.

Please see Appendix A for a review of the accumulated questionnaire data from the five CSPs.

7. Interviews

After having identified the five major CSPs, personal contacts were made to each for a request of a possible face-to-face interview. Upon their consent, interview sessions were arranged. The interviews were scheduled on dates that best suited the CSPs, took place in the company restaurant, and each lasted for an average of about half an hour. The interviewer took down notes verbatim as each CSP share their experiences. During the interview, attentive listening technique with minimal interruption was employed to encourage CSPs talk as much as possible.

8. Data Analysis

The results of the interviews were analyzed using content analysis. This technique is valuable for making "replicable and valid conclusions" (White & Marsh, 2006). [117] Talking with the CSPs during interview sessions, and asking them in-depth questions regarding their views, which they had expressed on the questionnaires helped the researcher validate their claims. That added more integrity to the validity of the information received.

9. Findings

The findings of this research are organized into various themes as stated below.

i. Ontology of the Subject Matter

All CSPs attested to the existence of workplace conflicts.

Ii. Frequency

---

[117] Ashkanasy, Hartel, and Zerbe, 21.

All participants experienced workplace conflicts at least twice a week.

iii. Socio-cultural Perspective

Conflict occurrence was very high between workers of different socio-cultural backgrounds (nationality, religion, language). A limited number of conflicts were found to occur between workers of the same social background.

iv. Workers' Interpersonal Relationship

The social and business relationship among co-workers and leaders was found to be not-so-good and not-so-bad. In the case study, all participants acknowledged their relationship with fellow co-workers to be *"So-so"*. While 40% of the participants attributed this to racial difference and co-worker insolence, 60% saw this mediocre worker relationship as a consequence of the respective personalities of individual workers.

v. The Main Cause of Conflict

The main cause of conflict was traced to workers' interpersonal skills. The way workers/leaders were spoken to, were addressed and regarded by other co-workers/co-leaders was found to be the spearing arrow that tore workers apart, destabilizing them from within.

vi. Conflict Effect (intrapersonal)

Most CSPs became somehow internally depressed as a result of workplace conflict. The reason for this social depression is that workers felt so much disrespected by their colleagues.

vii. Duration of Effect

While the effect of conflict lasted for only between two to three days for 40% of CSPs, as much as 60% attested that the malaise lingered in them for more than a month.

viii. Conflict Reaction

60% of CSPs reacted to workplace conflict by ignoring the opponent's actions and moving on while 40% reacted by confronting the latter (*fight*). As a reaction to the job, as much as 80% confessed they often willfully slowed down their performance (*fold*) following conflict sessions. With respect to resigning from the company (*flight*) due to conflict, 80% admitted they never had such an experience while 20% admitted they almost did.

I was particularly interested in the CSP who almost resigned his job due to conflict. During the interview, I wanted to find out from him what reason he had thought of putting forward to management if he were to resign. "Assume you did not reverse your decision to quit," I asked, "were you going to tell management exactly why you were to resign?" "No, no, no!" he exclaimed. "Why?" I asked.

"I just wanted to leave," he replied. "You know, I didn't want it to seem as if I was the trouble-maker. Also the guy I had a quarrel with was an old staff; I was just less than a year old in the company. So, I knew no matter how hard I could have tried to put forward my case, he would have still had an upper hand since I knew he was more valuable to the company than me, " he concluded.

ix. Performance Self-Rating

While 40% of CSPs confessed that there was no improvement in their performance during the conflict interval, as much as 60% attested that they could not tell if their performance declined or not during this period.

x. Management Intervention

While 80% of CSPs admitted there was no structure put in place by management to handle workplace conflicts, 20% said they had no knowledge whether such a system does exist or not. However, all participants did stress that management's intervention into workplace conflicts is a necessity. More than half (60%) of the participants, however, submitted that management should intervene only in special cases.

xi. Reason for Management Intervention

According to 80% of CSPs, management intervention is needed to prevent workplace conflict from further escalation and to restore organizational order. For the rest 20%, the intervention of management would help to guarantee the safety of workers and also increase their trust in management.

xii. Conflict Reporting

In conflict reporting, 20% of the CSPs proposed that management should design a system whereby employees are encouraged to report any workplace conflict immediately for management's prompt action. However, according to a majority (60%), management should rather design a conflict reporting form to be filled and submitted by an anonymous worker for security reasons. For the remaining 20%, leaders should talk to their workers as much as possible. This way they can easily know if any worker clash had occurred or not.

6.10 LIMITATIONS OF THE CASE STUDY

1. Sensitivity of the Subject Matter

So many limitations were encountered during the case study. Due to the very sensitive nature of the study, some CSPs were not as open as they would have been if the research were in a different subject. Since the research touches on the private lives of CSPs, I noticed how a CSP in the middle of the interview diverted from a point he was going to share only to wrap up the discussion with the plea, "Sorry, I don't have much time now. Can we talk at the same time tomorrow?" Even though I had taken the time in the very beginning of the project to explain to all five CSPs both in writing and in words that the exercise was purely for research purposes, and that no CSP's personal information would be given out to any third parties, I was nevertheless approached a day after the interview by a CSP to be assured once more that I was not going to reveal to the company management the information he had provided during the interview.

After talking and laughing on a different issue with a co-worker who had nothing to do with the research, the same troubled CSP approached me and asked, "What were you guys talking about?" The plague of fear had gripped him even after sharing how he felt in the company. This is true with most, if not all, workers.

Thus, from the experience of this fear-bound CSP, we can say that the sensitive nature of the subject matter made it almost impossible for the CSPs to be a hundred percent open to free and fair communication. However, we must strongly acknowledge that the testimonies that were obtained from the CSPs were far above satisfactory.

2. Time Factor

Time was also a critical factor that affected the smooth pace of the case study. Scheduling interviews outside of working hours was practically impossible as work lasted for some twelve hours. As a result, all interviews were conducted at work during lunch period. However, prior to the conduct of interviews, many interview dates had been cancelled and later rescheduled due to changes in the break period of either the CSP to be interviewed or researcher.

On the part of the researcher, working full-time and at the same time engaging on such a comprehensive research study was very challenging. Due to the length of working hours (twelve) per day, the researcher did not quite have sufficient time for re-writing and editing.

3. Language Proficiency

Another element that might have possibly hampered the research is language proficiency. Interviews with the two Japanese CSPs were conducted in Japanese, a language the researcher did not quite master like English. Therefore, the researcher presumes some vital information might have been lost during the interview process.

CHAPTER 7

CONCLUSION & RECOMMENDATIONS

7.1 Responding to Research Questions

It would be a great academic erratum to conclude our research project without making an assessment or evaluation of the research questions, the very essence or pillar upon which lies our research. We shall now restate the respective research questions, and, based on the findings from our study, give an evaluation of each:

- *Does workplace conflict hinder a worker's productivity?*

From our literature review, we saw a majority of the writers we contacted blacklisting conflict as the social predicament that must be dealt with if the organization and its entire system must function properly. To re-echo a few of these authors, Plato and Aristotle did stress that the absence of conflict is a sine qua non for the effective productivity of an organization (see page 10). For Elton Mayo, conflict is an evil that hampers the effectiveness of an organization. Thus, it must be minimized or totally eliminated if the organization must function properly (see page 11). On the impact of conflict on workers' productivity, Neuhauser writes, "Conflict is a major source of increased stress and decreased productivity for all managers and employees in any department of any organization." [118]

Turning towards our case study, the answer to the above question is a bold 'Yes' and a reserved 'No'. In this section, we shall elaborate on the 'Yes' response (please, see the paragraph below for the other part of the response). The case study carried out reveals that workplace conflict does, in a large number of cases, hinder workers' productivity. 40% of CSPs did confess that there was no improvement in their performance during the conflict interval. The other 60% could not really tell.

---

[118] Rahim, 2.

However, the observation phase of the case study seemed to have validated this claim. Standing at one end of the factory in close observance of one of the CSPs, I perceived a scene whereby the person in question appeared furious as he waved his right hand towards a co-worker in retaliation and was heading to the factory door. I approached him close to the door and asked what the problem was. His reply was, "I don't want to work with him anymore." Again I asked, "But what is the problem?" Leaving the door, he said, "He spoke to me very rudely. And he has been doing that often." He left only to return into the factory room some thirty minutes later. During the interval of his absence, the entire work allocated to that factory line could barely be accomplished. And even after his return, work wasn't as usual.

Clearly, there is a loss of productivity due to conflict. In this particular case I observed, there was at least thirty minutes of inactivity of labour due to conflict. No one probably took note of this fact save this researcher. In other organizations, depending on the situation, the time loss might be less or even more.

- *Can workplace conflict improve a worker's productivity?*

This question may seem quite absurd to many at face value. However, the findings from the case study reveal that workplace conflict has a limited potential in improving the performance of workers. Two of the CSPs indicated that the conflict they had with a few co-workers during work operations had challenged them to improve their performances.

In my interview with one of the CSPs, I asked, "Has any conflict during work operations in the past ever challenged you to seek better ways of improving your skills?" "Mmmmm," he muttered. "Yeah. I can think of one situation. When I was barely five months old in the company, I got entangled into a tussle with one co-worker that could have almost ended in a fight. Working together on the maintenance of the processing mill, the co-worker in question had requested me to turn on the pump switch for the drainage of the processing chemical waste that had settled in the processing mill. Moving towards the switch panel, there were three other switches in addition. Confused, I didn't know which was the right one to operate as I kept starring at the panel and asking myself, 'What do I do?' In the process, this guy rushed towards the panel, waved me aside and turned on the chemical drainage switch. I got really angry with his hostile and inconsiderate behavior as we both engaged in a verbal scuffle. The following day, I brought a small notebook to work where I noted the locations and purposes of the various switches. I think the conflict helped me to be more serious at work."

- *What should be done to prevent further loss of productivity and organizational disorder?*

When the kitchen section of an apartment building is on fire, to prevent the fire from spreading across the apartment rooms, all efforts must be directed towards the kitchen room that is ablaze, to extinguish it, and bring it under control. The same is true for strives, scuffles, combats, and disputes that occur among co-workers. Like the fire in the kitchen room, conflict between co-workers must be extinguished to prevent it from spreading into the entire organization. To perform such task requires a leadership that puts workers first, a leadership that assumes the great responsibility of liberating its workers through an immediate and tactful management of workplace conflicts for better worker productivity and organizational order.

As the society becomes more and more globalized with the Americans, Japanese, Australians, Italians, Sri Lankans, Bangladeshis, Kenyans, you name the rest, coming together to work as a team in their organization of employment, and with other third party organizations, the probability of workplace conflict to occur among these people having quite different socio-cultural backgrounds seems very high. And when this (conflict) occurs, it is the organization that shoulders the cost – loss of productivity and instability of the organization.

In the case study, all CSPs indicated that management intervention into workers' conflict was highly solicited. The reason given for such intervention was that it would help restore workers' broken relations, strengthen ties, and prevent conflicts from spilling over the entire organization. However, a cross section of CSPs maintained that management intervention was necessary only in specific cases. Intervention was not quite necessary in mild cases where disputants could sort out themselves, they claim.

7.2 A Final Conclusion

I heard some news over a radio network in Cameroon of how a huge pothole in one of the roads in Zimbabwe saved a dying child. The child in question had swallowed a marula seed that got stuck in her throat. As the child was being rushed to the hospital by her desperate parents, the vehicle inadvertently went into a pothole in one of the roads in Harare. The suddenness of the accident jolted the child off the seat as the child's head hit the roof of the car. This bizarre incidence fortunately forced the marula seed out of her throat. So, the pothole effectively saved the child.

Far from justifying why potholes should exist in our highways, the reporter commented, this story rather draws attention to the bad state of our roads. Our roads, most of which are in such a state, the reporter continued, have killed thousands in Cameroon just as they have done in Zimbabwe and elsewhere in Africa.

In this project, we have presented both sides of the conflict coin – its merits and demerits. We have shown how this social phenomenon does weaken workers' motivation to work and how it injects into the workforce a spirit of hate, backbiting, and melancholy, all of which by transforming the organization into a den similar to that of roaring lions, do no good in forging the organization ahead.

On the other hand, we have also shown how conflict does help workers understand and respect the values of their fellow co-workers by avoiding the latter's zone of discomfort. Likewise, we have shown, among others, how conflict, in certain cases, does motivate conflicting parties to improve their commitments.

Therefore, having a full mastery of what conflict is and what it can do in our organization will empower us to draft effective measures to kick it out of our organization and preserve the organizational image and output.

Going back to the story of the little girl who swallowed the marula seed, should we say that because the pothole saved the girl's life, every pothole in our roads must be left untarred? I guess you would agree with me that the answer is an unequivocal 'No.' In the same manner, while acknowledging some of the benefits that could come along with workplace conflicts, we must not forget, as has been shown throughout this paper, that conflict does to an organization more harm than good. Therefore, all efforts must be made to tackle this social phenomenon tactfully so as to heal the broken wounds of the organization's workforce for better productivity and organizational order.

7.3 Recommendations

Following the findings that were obtained from this research, the following recommendations have been made:

1. Comply with Organizational Culture

"Nature to be commanded must be obeyed," was a famous statement made by Francis Bacon (New Organon: The True Directions Concerning the Interpretations of Nature, III), one of the greatest intellectuals the world has had. To be in full command of the organization's business and its work milieu, the organizational culture, the socio-economic vein through which the business of the organization flows, must be duly observed by both management staff as well as their employees. In case of its defilement, it must be reinforced.

It is the culture of an organization that gives life to that organization, thereby motivating workers' day-to-day actions. When workers fully observe the norms and values that define the way in which an organization's business should be run, workplace conflicts and other workplace-related incidences will be at their minimum. The case study does reveal that most conflicts occur due to the fact that one or both conflicting parties failed to pay respect to the business norms of the organization.

2. Know Your Employees:

Consequently, employers and managers of labor must create quality time to know exactly what is happening around their business places and with their employees in particular.

3. Create Watchdog Intervention Unit:

To effect the above, a watchdog intervention unit, which specializes in overseeing on-duty social problems that workers do encounter, should be created as a specialized arm of the Human Resource department.

4. Test Workers' Interpersonal Skills:

Prior to recruitment, the interpersonal skills of potential candidates should be thoroughly tested. This point needs to be given a serious consideration as workers' poor interpersonal skills have been shown by our case study to constitute the root cause of workplace conflicts.

It is true that employers these days tend to focus more on the work capabilities of candidates than on their social skills or abilities to work effectively with others. They focus on what these candidates can deliver ignoring what they could ruin. The question that employers of labour, leaders, and managers are called upon to ask themselves is this: Must we sacrifice the smooth and serene working atmosphere in our organizations for the output of a skilled worker who barely values either the culture of the organization or its moral obligations objective expected from workers?

5. Ungroup Socially Incompatible Workers

We are told by the magnificent science of chemistry that whenever certain chemicals are mixed (or even stored together) with others from a different compatibility group, chaos does occur. As an example, when acetone comes into contact with the air, an explosive mixture is formed. Also, acetone reacts violently with activated charcoal, chloroform, aliphatic amines, bromine, bromine trifluoride, chlorotriazine, iodoform, peroxomonosulphuric acid, hexachloromelamine, [119] to name these few. Also note that when acetone comes into contact with most rubber, resins, and plastics (polyethylenes, polyester, vinylester, PVC, Neoprene, Viton), there is a very high probability that these substances would be completely dissolved." [120]

Just like acetone is incompatible with certain chemical substances, in the same manner, some workers would find it difficult to work with other specific workers without incurring personal damages. Therefore, managers, leaders, and employers of labour are called upon to carefully identify within each department unit workers that are socially incompatible, ungroup, and regroup them with workers they can go along with to prevent any unforeseen contingencies.

6. Train Corporate Leaders on Human Resource Management

One of the major factors that were identified to contribute to workplace conflicts was the poor personnel management

---

[119] Richard P. Pohanish and Stanley A. Greene, *Wiley Guide to Chemical Incompatibilities,* 2nd ed. (USA: John Wiley & Sons, Inc., 2003), 16.
[120] Ibid., 16.

skills of leaders. Most of the leaders in the manufacturing department of the company under case study albeit experts in the engineering sector had little or no education and experience on Human Resource Management. Consequently, they acted in ways that, in most cases, only ended up bruising their workers. As one writer rightly said, "Every leader is a manager of human resource." Therefore, anyone appointed to a post of responsibility irrespective of the job title should be adequately trained to better manage the people under his/her unit of service.

7. Standardize all Work Procedures/methods:

When organizational norms and procedures/methods for carrying out work operations vary from worker to worker, it creates a potential conflict and weakens organizational control. During the observation phase of this research, I discovered that although a significant proportion of the work methods in the factory had been harmonized, there were still a few cases where workers could be seen devising their own methods of executing the job. Most of this created discords among workers especially those who did not share that particular work method for one reason or another.

REFERENCES

Anderson, Valerie
    2004 Research Methods in Human Resource Management. UK: CIPD House.

Anolli, Luigi, Starkey Duncan Jr., Magnus S. Magnusson, and Giuseppe Riva, eds.
    2005 The Hidden Structure of Interaction: From Neurons to Culture Patterns. Amsterdam: IOS Press.

Ashkanasy, Neal M., Charmine E.J. Hartel, and Wilfred J. Zerbe, eds.
    2012 Research on Emotion in Organizations: Experiencing and Managing Emotions in the Workplace. (Vol. 8). UK: Emerald Group Publishing Ltd.

Avruch, Kevin
    1998 Culture and Conflict Resolution. Washington: United States Institute of Peace Press.

Bacon, Francis
    2000 The New Organon. Lisa Jardine and Michael Silverthorne, eds. UK: Cambridge University Press.

    2010 [1620] The New Organon: The True Directions Concerning the Interpretations of Nature. MobileReference. http://books.google.co.jp/books?id=hTbE_UHvWg8C&print sec=frontcover#v=onepage&q&f=false

Baron-Cohen, Simon, ed.
    1997 The Maladapted Mind: Classic Readings in Evolutionary Psychopathology. UK: Psychology Press.

Berman, Jacquelin and Lisa M. Furst
    2011 Depressed Older Adults: Education and Screening.
    New York: Springer Publishing Company, LLC.

Bertocci, David I.
    2009 Leadership in Organizations: There is a Difference
    between Leaders and Managers. Maryland: University
    Press of America.

Bhattacharyya, Dipak Kumar
    2006 Research Methodology. (2nd ed.). New Delhi: Excel
    Books.

Bryman, Alan, David Collinson, Keith Grint, Mary Uhl-Bien, and
    Brad Jackson, eds.
    2011 The SAGE Handbook of Leadership. London: SAGE
    Publications Ltd.

Buckley, William R. and Cathy J. Okrent
    2004 Torts & Personal Injury Law. (3rd ed.). Canada:
    Thomson Delmar Learning.

Cargan, Leonard
    2007 Doing Social Research. USA: Rowman & Littlefield
    Publishers, Inc.

Clutterbuck, David and Sheila Hirst
    2002 Talking Business: Making Communication Work.
    UK: The Item Group Ltd.

Cohen, Louis, Lawrence Manion, and Keith Morison
    2011 Research Methods in Education. England: Routledge.

Colbert, Don
    2003 Deadly Emotions: Understand the Mind-Body-Spirit
    Connection that can Heal or Destroy You. Nashville:
    Thomas Nelson, Inc.

Coombs, Clyde H. and George S. Avrunin
       1988 The Structure of Conflict. New Jersey: Lawrence
       Erlbaum Associates, Inc.

Cooper, Terry D.
       2003 Sin, Pride & Self-Acceptance: The Problem of
       Identity in Theology & Psychology. USA: Inter Varsity
       Press.

Cowan, David
       2003 Taking Charge of Organizational Conflict: A Guide to
       Managing Anger and Confrontation. USA: Personhood
       Press.

Crum, Thomas
       1987 The Magic of Conflict: Turning a Life of Work into a
       Work of Art. USA: Touchstone.

Darwin, Charles
       2007 The Expression of the Emotions in Man and Animals.
       Teddington: The Echo Library.

       2010 The Origin of Species by Means of Natural Selection.
       Madison: Cricket House Books, LLC.

De Dreu, Carsten K. W., and Bianca Beersma, eds.
       2005 Conflict in Organizations: Beyond Effectiveness and
       Performance. UK: Psychology Press Ltd.

Donohue, William A. and Robert Colt
       1992 Managing Interpersonal Conflict. California: Sage
       Publications Inc.

Feagin, Joe R., Anthony M. Orum, and Gideon Sjoberg
       1991 A Case for the Case Study. USA: The University of
       North Carolina Press.

Fellows, Richard F. and Anita Liu
    2008 Research Methods for Construction. UK: Blackwell Publishing Ltd.

Freire, Paulo
    2006 Pedagogy of the Oppressed: 30th Anniversary Edition. Myra Bergman Ramos, trans. New York: Continuum Int'l Pub. Group Inc.

Gerzon, Mark
    2006 Leading through Conflict: How Successful Leaders Transform Differences into Opportunities. USA: Harvard Business School Press.

Gillham, Bill
    2000 Case Study Research Methods. London: Continuum.

Greener, Sue
    2008 Business Research Methods. UK: Dr. Sue Greener & Ventus Publishing ApS.

Guerin, Lisa
    2007 The Essential Guide to Workplace Investigations. USA: Nolo.

Haslam, S. Alexander, Stephen D. Reicher, and Michael J. Platow
    2011 The New Psychology of Leadership: Identity, Influence and Power. England: Psychology Press.

Heymann, Sally J.
    2010 Profit at the Bottom of the Ladder: Creating Value by Investing in Your Workforce. USA: Harvard Business Press.

Hodgkinson, Christopher
    1991 Educational Leadership: The Moral Art. USA: State University of New York Press.

Jonker, Jan and Bartjan Pennink
    2010 The Essence of Research Methodology: A Concise
    Guide for Master and PhD Students in Management Science.
    Heidelberg: Springer.

Kelly, Matthew
    2007 The Dream Manager. USA: Beacon Publishing.

Knapp, Mark L. and John A. Daly, eds.
    2002 Handbook of Interpersonal Communication. (3rd ed.).
    USA: Sage Publications, Inc.

Kolb, Deborah and Jean Bartunek, eds.
    1992 Hidden Conflict in Organizations: Uncovering
    Behind-the-Scenes Disputes. California: Sage Publications
    Inc.

Kothari, C. R.
    2004 Research Methodology: Methods and Techniques.
    (2nd ed.). New Delhi: New Age Int'l Publishers.

Kumar, Ranjit
    2011 Research Methodology: A Step-by-step Guide for
    Beginners. (3rd ed.). London: SAGE Publications Ltd.

Lane, Richard D. and Lynn Nadel, eds.
    2000 Cognitive Neuroscience of Emotion. New York:
    Oxford University Press, Inc.

Lawler, Jennifer.
    2010 "The Real Cost of Workplace Conflict: How Much
    Office Drama Cuts into Your Bottom Line," Entrepreneur.
    Accessed December 30, 2013.
    http://www.entrepreneur.com/article/207196

Lehman, Carol M. and Debbie D. Dufrene
    2010 Business Communication. (16th ed.). USA: Cengage
    Learning, 2010), 4.

Lynn, Adele B
        2000 50 Activities for Developing Emotional Intelligence.
        Amherst: HRD Press.

Matyok, Thomas, Jessica Seneyi, and Sean Byrne
        2011 Critical Issues in Peace and Conflict Studies: Theory,
        Practice, and Pedagogy. USA: Rowman & Littlefield
        Education.

McBurney, Donald H. and Theresa L. White
        2010 Research Methods. (8th ed.). USA: Wadsworth.

Michail, Antonios
        2011 An Investigation of the Relationship between Value
        Chain Activities and Generic Strategies in Small and
        Medium-sized Enterprises in UK Manufacturing. (Doctoral
        Thesis). Germany: GRIN Verlag.

Miller, Roger LeRoy and William Eric Hollowell
        2011 Business Law: Text & Exercises. (6th ed.). USA:
        Cengage Learning.

Nicotera , Anne Maydan, ed.
        1995 Conflict and Organizations: Communicative
        Processes. Albany: State University of New York Press.

Oade, Aryanne
        2009 Managing Workplace Bullying: How to Identify,
        Respond to and Manage Bullying Behaviour in the
        Workplace. UK: Palgrave Macmillan.

Parrott, W. Gerrod, ed.
        2001 Emotions in Social Psychology: Essential Readings.
        USA: Psychology Press.

Plessner, Henning, Cornelia Betsch, and Tilmann Betsch, eds.
        2010 Intuition in Judgment and Decision Making. USA:
        Taylor & Francis Group, LLC.

Pohanish, Richard P. and Stanley A. Greene
        2003 Wiley Guide to Chemical Incompatibilities. (2nd ed.).
        USA: John Wiley & Sons, Inc.

Prokopenko, Joseph
        1987 Productivity Management: A Practical Handbook.
        Geneva: Int'l Labour Office.

Rahim, M. Afzalur, ed.
        2001 Managing Conflict in Organizations. USA:
        Greenwood Publishing Group.

Samovar, Larry A., Richard E. Porter, Edwin R. McDaniel, and
        Carolyn S. Roy
        2010 Communication Between Cultures. (7th ed.). Canada:
        Wadsworth, Cengage Learning.

Sashkin, Marshall and Molly G. Sashkin
        2003 Leadership that Matters: The Critical Factors for
        Making a Difference in People's Lives and Organizations'
        Success. USA: Berrett-Koehler Publishers, Inc.

Taylor, Bill, Gautam Sinha, and Taposh Ghoshal
        2006 Research Methodology: A Guide for Researchers in
        Management and Social Sciences. New Delhi: Prentice-
        Hall of India Private Ltd.

Tidwell, Alan C.
        1998 Conflict Resolved?: A Critical Assessment of
        Conflict Resolution. London: Continuum.

Yin, Robert K.
        2009 Case Study Research: Design and Methods. (4th ed.).
        USA: SAGE Publications Inc.

Appendix A

Case Study Questionnaire Data

Q1: Have you ever encountered workplace conflicts?				
CSP1	**CSP2**	**CSP3**	**CSP4**	**CSP5**
Yes	Yes	Yes	Yes	Yes
Q2: How often?				
Once/week	Once/week	Once/week	Once/week	Once/week
Q3: Are you of the same regional and cultural background?				
No/A few	No/A few	No/A few	No	No
Q:4 What led to the conflict?				
The leader/co-worker spoke to me in a rude manner	Same as CSP 1	Same as CSP 1	Same as CSP 1	Same as CSP 1
Q5: What was the first thing that came to your mind?				
Will relax performance	Same as CSP 1	Same as CSP 1	Will fight back	Same as CSP 4
Q6: How did it affect you?				
I felt depressed	I felt dis-respected	Same as CSP 2	Same as CSP 2	Same as CSP 2
Q7: For how long did the conflict tension last?				
More than 1 month	Same as CSP 1	1-3 days	Same as CSP 3	Same as CSP 1

Appendix A Cont'd

Q8: **How did you rate your performance during the conflict interval?**				
CSP 1	**CSP 2**	**CSP 3**	**CSP 4**	**CSP 5**
No change	Declined	Can't tell	Same as CSP 3	Same as CSP 3
Q:9: **Why did it improve, decline, or not change?**				
I ignored my co-worker's actions	I was de-motivated	N/A	N/A	N/A
Q10: **Is there a management system for handling conflicts in your company?**				
No	No.	I don't know	No	No
Q:11: **Is management intervention needed?**				
Somehow needed	Same as CSP 1	Same as CSP 1	Same as CSP 1	Greatly needed
Q12: **Why is management intervention needed/not needed?**				
To prevent conflict from further escalation and restore order	Same as CSP 1	To guarantee workers' safety and trust in management	Same as CSP 1	Same as CSP 1
Q13: **How can management be made aware of employee conflict?**				
Employees should report conflict cases to management	Management should draft a conflict reporting form to be completed by an anonymous	The leader talks to workers as much as possible	Same as CSP 2	Same as CSP 2

Q14: Should management always intervene in conflict issues?				
CSP 1	**CSP 2**	**CSP 3**	**CSP 4**	**CSP 5**
In special cases only	Same as CSP 1	Same as CSP 1	Yes, it should	Same as CSP 4
Q15: Why or why not?				
To prevent conflict escalation and to restore order	Same as CSP 1	To guarantee workers' safety and company trust	Same as CSPs 1 & 3	Same as CSP 1
Q16: How is your work relationship with co-workers?				
So-So	Good	So-So	So-So	So-So
Q17: Could you give us a reason?				
Some troublesome workers left	Work seems a bit better	N/A	Coworker Insolence	Racial difference
Q18: How do you often react to conflict?				
I ignore the opponent and move on	Same as CSP 1	I abandon the task and face the opponent	Same as CSP 1	Same as CSP 3
Q19: How do you resist or resolve conflict?				
I ignore the opponent's comments	I painfully satisfy the opponent's request	Same as CSP 2	Same as CSP 2	Same as CSP 1
Q20: What do you do when in conflict?				
I remain calm	I complain to other people	Same as CSP 2	Same as CSPs 1 & 2	I scream at the other party
Q21: Have you ever resigned due to conflict				
Never	Never	Almost	Never	Never

Appendix A Cont'd

Q22: If yes, what reason did you give?				
CSP 1	**CSP2**	**CSP 3**	**CSP 4**	**CSP 5**
N/A	N/A	I gave a different reason	N/A	N/A
Q23: What other factors make you not want to work together with certain people?				
They hardly greet / They lack respect for others	They lack respect for others	Same as CSP 2	They over-impose on others	Same as CSP 2
Q24: What are the other factors that make you depressed at work?				
None in particular	N/A	Overtime work	N/A	Same as CSP 3
Q25: What should be in place for you to consider working in the company for a lifetime?				
Good relationship with coworkers	Same as CSP 1	Promotion and incentives	Same as CSPs 1 & 3	Same as CSP 1

Appendix B

An Account from a CEO

The Real Cost of Workplace Conflict

When Rory Rowland, then CEO of a small financial institution, encountered a petty workplace conflict between two of his employees--"I don't even remember what it was about, but it was over an insignificant matter, like the way one of them looked at the other"--he didn't immediately address the problem.

That turned out to be a big mistake. "It escalated to the point where they were snarling at each other. They weren't professional at all. They would just fling [stuff] at each other's work area." This might be funny when it's on a sitcom, but not when it's happening in your business.

While every small-business owner knows that such workplace conflicts affect productivity and morale, the hard money drain of office drama is not as obvious. When CPP Inc.--publishers of the Myers-Briggs Assessment and the Thomas-Kilmann Conflict Mode Instrument--commissioned a study on workplace conflict, they found that in 2008, U.S. employees spent 2.8 hours per week dealing with conflict. This amounts to approximately \$359 billion in paid hours (based on average hourly earnings of \$17.95), or the equivalent of 385 million working days.

That's a lot of time spent gossiping, protecting turf, retaliating, recruiting people to one side or the other, planning defenses and navigating the drama. More importantly, that's time not spent answering customer questions, filling orders or doing the job employees were hired to do.

"It was impacting the entire organization," Rowland says of the conflict at his company. "People had to navigate around them. I found out later that the two employees were recruiting people to take their sides."

Even customers took notice and complained to Rowland. "They said, 'You have some snarky employees.' If you're [angry], it's tough to be all smiles. We didn't lose customers, but it impacted our image, and I hated that."

Now a speaker and consultant for financial institutions and the author of *My Best Boss Ever*, Rowland says the most important thing in dealing with workplace conflict is to "recognize that ripping the bandage off is painful, but after it's done everything is all better."

How did Rowland rip off the bandage? "I had the two employees come in and put it on the table. I told them we weren't going to quit until the issue was resolved. One of the techniques I used was you couldn't restate your own position until you stated the other person's position to their approval. When you're angry and hurt, the last thing you want to do is restate the other person's perspective." This forced both employees to step out of their own complaints and look at the other side.

The meeting took several hours, and afterward the two changed their ways. "They said they would rather be polite than go back to what they called 'the chamber' again," Rowland says. Neither was fired, and both continued with the company for the long term.

For Rowland, the cost wasn't in just the actual number of hours it took to solve the problem and in the negative effect it had on the workplace and on customers. "I wasted a tremendous amount of time hoping it would go away; I was wrong."

Conflict Is Costly

Findings from the CPP study should be enough to spur any "wait and see" business owner into action. For example, 25 percent of employees said that avoiding conflict led to sickness or absence from work. Equally alarming, nearly 10 percent reported that workplace conflict led to project failure and more than one-third said that conflict resulted in someone leaving the company, either through firing or quitting.

Those negatives translate into real financial losses for small businesses.

If a worker uses five sick days a year to avoid conflict, that's a direct cost of over $700 to your business (calculated using the above hourly earnings), not to mention the cost of covering the employee's missed work (e.g., overtime pay for another worker or hiring a temporary employee). Multiply that by 50 workers, or even 10, and you can immediately see the kind of money drain conflict creates.

Employee turnover owing to conflict is also expensive. Consider the costs of filling a vacant position: recruitment costs (including everything from placing ads to hiring head hunters), training the new hire, paying other employees involved in the hiring and training process, paying severance, and the lost investment you made in the previous employee (including their knowledge). Replacing an employee will cost you 150 to 200 percent more than that employee's salary and benefits. This means that losing even a mid-level employee making $30,000 a year could cost your company $70,000 or more to replace.

(Source: Jennifer Lawler, "The Real Cost of Workplace Conflict: How Much Office Drama Cuts into Your Bottom Line," *Entrepreneur* (June 2010), accessed December 30, 2013, http://www.entrepreneur.com/article/207196).

Appendix C

Sample Complaint Policy

Our company is committed to providing a safe and productive work environment, free of threats to the health, safety, and well-being of our workers. Such threats might include, but are not limited to, harassment, discrimination, violations of health and safety rules, and violence.

Any employee who witnesses or is subject to inappropriate conduct in the workplace may complain to _____________ or to any company officer. Any supervisor, manager, or company officer who receives a complaint about, hears of, or witnesses any inappropriate conduct is required to immediately notify _____________. Inappropriate conduct includes any conduct prohibited by our company policies about harassment, discrimination, discipline, workplace violence, health and safety, wages and hours, and drug and alcohol use. In addition, we encourage employees to come forward with any workplace complaint, even if the subject of the complaint is not explicitly covered by our written policies.

We encourage you to come forward with complaints immediately, so we can take whatever action is needed to handle the problem. Once a complaint has been made, _____________ will determine how to handle it. For serious complaints, we will immediately conduct a complete and impartial investigation.

We expect all employees to cooperate fully in company investigations by, for example, answering questions completely and honestly and giving the investigator all documents and other material that might be relevant. All complaints will be handled as confidentially as possible. When the investigation is complete, the company will take corrective action, if appropriate.

The company will not engage in or allow retaliation against any employee who makes a good-faith complaint or participates in an investigation. If you believe that you are being subjected to any kind of negative treatment because you made or were questioned about a complaint, report the conduct immediately to ______________.

Source: Lisa Guerin, *The Essential Guide to Workplace Investigations* (USA: Nolo, 1964), 319.

Appendix D

Caution: Do not be Overwhelmed with the Complainant's Emotions

If the Complaining Employee is Unhappy

Even if you take immediate and effective action against the wrongdoer, the complaining employee may be upset. Perhaps the complaining employee believes a harsher punishment should have been imposed, has suffered damage to reputation and/or work opportunities because of the complaint, or does not believe the wrongdoer will shape up.

Your company is under no obligation to impose the punishment your complaining employee favors. Your obligation is to the company, the accused employee, and the rest of your workforce to be fair and reasonable. However, you should listen carefully to the complaining employee's concerns. Perhaps the employee who claims that the wrongdoer will never change is worried about retaliation or further misconduct. If so, you can assure the complaining employee that you will deal swiftly with any such behavior. An employee who claims to have suffered because of the misconduct may have a point: If the employee was unfairly denied a promotion, raise, or time off, for example, you should consider conferring these benefits retroactively.

Although complaining employees may well have their own axes to grind, they can also help you figure out whether you have chosen an effective remedy. If the resolution you've chosen isn't going to work, better to hear about it now when you can fix the problem than later in a lawsuit.

Source: Lisa Guerin, *The Essential Guide to Workplace Investigations* (USA: Nolo, 1964), 103.

APPENDIX E

Some Cases of Workplace Conflicts

A- Violence

- "Honeywell, Inc., decided to rehire Randy Landin as a custodian – after he was released from prison, having served five years for strangling a Honeywell coworker to death. After he was rehired, Landin sexually harassed female coworkers, challenged a male coworker to a fight, and threatened to kill another coworker – he was transferred twice because of these confrontations. After a female coworker spurned his romantic overtures, he harassed and threatened her, scratched a death threat on her locker door at work, then shot and killed her. *Yunker v. Honeywell, Inc.,* 496 NW2d 419 (Minn. Ct. of Apps., 1993)." [121]

B- Harassment

Harassment is defined as any workplace mistreatment of a worker that is based on the worker's protected characteristics.

---

[121] Guerin, 274.

[122] Protected characteristics may include race, colour, region of origin, sex, age, disability, religion, etc.

The three examples cited below constitute cases of harassment. [123]

- "A Jewish officer worker is subjected to jokes about the Holocaust and is assigned to a bookkeeping position because 'Jews know how to handle money.'"

- An African-American salesman works at a car dealership. His coworkers make racist comments about nonwhite customers; after he tell them that he finds their comments offensive, they start referring to themselves jokingly as "the KKK."

- A clerical worker with cerebral palsy is mimicked by her supervisor, who ridicules her speech and the way she walks, blames her for errors she did not commit, and tells her coworkers that she is incompetent "but we can't fire her because she's disabled."

---

[122] Guerin, 175.
[123] Ibid.

Appendix F

Differences between Managers and Leaders

Managers	Leaders
✓ Managers are driven by a desire for order and regularity, opting for incremental change and marginal improvements.	✓ Leaders are restless spirits, unwilling to leave well-enough alone, eager to bring about large-scale change and improvement.
✓ Managers view efficiency as one of their supreme objectives, reducing waste and always trying to do a thousand things slightly better.	✓ Leaders, on the other hand, do not mind disorder and waste, which they often view as a price that must be paid in order to achieve change. NB: Waste can be waste of materials, waste of time and other resources and even the loss of human life.
✓ Managers are keenly aware that details can be important; they seek to eliminate uncertainty by carefully weighing out options and taking care of details.	✓ Leaders are often driven by a vision of the future which is broad and general. They generally do not enjoy looking at details and making careful plans for all contingencies. They often disregard important details, which can derail the overall project.
✓ Correspondingly, managers are generally smart people operating logically and valuing rationality above all else. They look carefully at information, costs, benefits and risks before making decisions and view emotion as a disruptive and dangerous force.	✓ Leaders, on the other hand, often operate at an emotional level, stirring up emotions in their followers and exciting emotions in themselves. Logic is often eclipsed by intuition, hunches, and gut feelings. Instead of careful consideration of all possible alternatives, leaders often commit themselves to an alternative that contains uncertainties and risks, but also hidden possibilities.

Adapted from *The SAGE Handbook of Leadership*, Bryman et al., eds.

ABOUT THE AUTHOR

Njikang Clovis Mebinaji is a charismatic and passionate solution-oriented thinker whose life ambition is to teach, defend, and orient men and women towards literature that emancipates them from the troubles of our fallen world. He hails from Cameroon and is the 13th child in a polygamous family of 17. He holds two doctorate degrees, one in Theology, the other in Religious Education. He also holds an International Master in Business Administration (IMBA), a bachelor of art in Theology and a bachelor of science in Accountancy. Mebinaji is happily married to Catherine, and they have a daughter, Mebilyn.